To Chris, christmas 1985. With much love Dad.

WHAT THIS HANDBOOK IS ALL ABOUT

The Practicalities and Realities of Finding Jobs in Hawaii

Job Sources
Current Labor Market Information
Job Trends
Occupations which need Licensing
Businesses and Industries
Unemployment Trends
Job Search Approaches
Self-Assessment/Self-Inventory
Communication Process
Letters of Application
Resumes
Job Interviews — How and Why
Barriers to Employment
Federal and State Employment Laws
Federal and State Enforcement Agencies
Discussion of the terms Minorities and Disadvantaged

JOB SEARCHING IN HAWAII

PRACTICALITIES AND REALITIES

By
Adam P. Y. Lim

PRESS PACIFICA

1978

Library of Congress Cataloging in Publication Data

Lim, Adam P Y 1925-
Job Searching in Hawaii.

Bibliography: 192p.
1. Vocational guidance – Hawaii. 2. Job vacancies – Hawaii. 3. Labor supply – Hawaii. 4. Applications for positions. I. Title.
HF5382.5.U6H34 1978 650'.14'09969 77-83968
ISBN 0-916630-06-4

Cover design by David Pultz

REVISED EDITION

ISBN 0-916630-06-4
Library of Congress Catalog Card Number 77-83968

Manufactured in the United States of America by R.R. Donnelley & Sons Company

PRESS PACIFICA / P.O.Box 47 / Kailua, HI 96734

TO:

My Precious Four

Kari, Ann, Kathy & Michael

PREFACE

Teaching the job seeker approaches to job hunting is not novel. A good deal has been written about this subject, but usually, the literature has dealt with limited topical matters, has been general in treatment, or has been directed towards special audiences. This handbook is unique in that the delivery of the subject matter and methodology is comprehensive, compact, practical, realistic, relevant to all, and focuses on job searching in Hawaii.

Looking for work in Hawaii is a constant and on-going process. This handbook is designed for the person who desires work in Hawaii and who wants to facilitate finding the job. It is intended to alert the job candidate of the practicalities and realities necessary in job searching.

This handbook will provide the reader with basic labor/occupational information, with an understanding of the aspects and mechanics of job seeking, and with the various applications of this basic knowledge so as to assure more success in job searching in Hawaii than would be otherwise.

Essentially, the handbook guides the reader to systematically analyze acquired personal skills, to inventory related and unrelated work potential, and to apply these assets realistically to the present labor market in Hawaii.

Education, work training, work experience and other assets will add to and enhance the job seeker's personal skill, knowledge and chances for a job. Vocational counseling and career planning will broaden an individual's insight in and awareness of the world of work. Job referrals will help to some extent, but in view of competitiveness for jobs and selectivity on the part of employers, these assets may be inadequate for placement in the job market. Difficulties are encountered, especially by those with less verbal, social and saleable skills, or by those who are disadvantaged in one way or another due to physical appearance, cultural differences, age, sex; physical, mental, social disabilities, lack of influence, and different life-styles, or by being a newcomer to the community, being unqualified, being long-term unemployed and being recently discharged from military service.

It is indeed a naive point of view to believe that possession of an educational or occupational degree, certificate, and even experience and skills is a passport to employment – that employment is an automatic process, or that somehow an individual is absorbed into the labor market with ease. The tight labor market condition in Hawaii breeds selectivity, competitiveness and provincialism, and these are the realities which the job searcher encounters.

Prolonged direct assistance from others is limited for most, and within the confines of this limitation, the job seeker becomes aware of cold facts – that jobs have to be sought out and that when employer contacts are made, the job seeker is alone.

Knowledge of job search preparation will strengthen an individual's job hunting skills. In essence, this handbook attempts to provide the individual with data and encouragement to reinforce self-confidence in locating job sources and making employer contacts. It is also designed to help the job seeker to be self-reliant, to acquire meaningful job seeking knowledge, to do what has to be done, and to apply all personal resources systematically and positively in securing employment.

While conditions for seeking employment in Hawaii are less than ideal, it is hoped that this handbook will provide realistic and practical means for assisting, encouraging and reinforcing the individual in job seeking.

TABLE OF CONTENTS

ACKNOWLEDGEMENTS

Sincerest acknowledgement is extended to Dr. Greta Kilpinen, faculty member of Leeward Community College, for her arduous labors in reviewing this handbook and making valuable contributions toward improvement in clarity and format.

To Leslie Munro and Elena Bumanglag, also faculty members of Leeward Community College, for reviewing portions of this handbook and suggesting improvements.

To Gloria Grier, Assistant Equal Employment Coordinator of the University of Hawaii, Manoa Campus, for reviewing parts of this handbook and recommending improvement in clarity and factuality.

To Jocelyn O. Burns, Registrar of a State Community College, for reviewing many portions of this handbook and making valuable contributions toward clarity and contents.

To Ray A. Ziegler - wherever you are, Mahalo for your enthusiasm radiated, good wishes extended, encouragement given and knowledge shared with respect to your Creative Job Search Techniques style of delivery.

...... And to the countless of thousands of job seekers interviewed by the author who have contributed to the experience, knowledge and substance which made this handbook possible.

CHAPTER 1

JOB SOURCES IN HAWAII

Knowledge of job sources is vital to you as a job seeker, especially if you are unaware of the resources in the locale or community of your job search. Job sources provide you with specific and general job leads and information covering many types of occupations. Some of these leads and informational sources may prove useful while others may not. This depends on your circumstances, personal situation, interests, and needs.

In Hawaii, the job applicant has access to various categories of job sources which offer jobs, as well as job referrals, job leads and job information. No matter how these job sources are categorized - whether these be basic, primary or secondary sources, the important point to remember is that numerous resources are accessible within the community and that jobs, job leads and/or information about them are available when these sources are tapped. For the purpose of simple categorization, these resources are:

1) Governmental agency sources which directly offer jobs, give referrals, and provide job information.
2) Agency and institutional sources which provide indirect job referrals or information.
3) Job sources, printed and publicized, which provide job leads and information.
4) Personnel offices of agencies, institutions, private firms, unions, small business establishments, the

military, and private employment agencies which offer jobs.

5) Professional associations, community associations, church groups, clubs, fraternal organizations, and other sources which provide job leads and influence.
6) People who provide job leads, information, and influence.

First of all, where and how do you obtain information about employment?

GOVERNMENTAL AGENCY SOURCES WHICH DIRECTLY OFFER JOBS, GIVE REFERRALS, AND PROVIDE JOB INFORMATION

There are numerous Hawaii governmental agencies which are concerned with employment in one way or another, and these should be basic sources in job seeking. Governmental agencies *do not* charge fees for referral or placement assistance. These are tax supported agencies, and job seekers can contact these agencies directly. However, job seekers should be aware of a one-year residency requirement which must be met in order to seek jobs with the state or county governments.*

HAWAII STATE EMPLOYMENT SERVICE

The Hawaii State Employment Service (HSES) provides job placement and other related services to the general public. The services offered are similar in each of the HSES offices and are primarily aimed at helping job applicants. This free State service has five placement offices on Oahu which assist job applicants according to geographical or zip code districts. (except for the WIN Office).** The five offices are the Honolulu Office, the Waipahu Office, the Kaneohe Office, the Kalihi Office, and the WIN Office. The WIN Office provides

---

*Act 211, a law recently enacted by the Ninth Legislature, Regular Session of 1977, State of Hawaii, imposed this one-year residency requirement. (It could be subject to change.) Since interpretation and application of this Law can vary, job seekers should make certain that they meet this requirement prior to applying for jobs with the various state and county agencies.

**Work Incentive Program.

placement services to Aid to Families with Dependent Children (AFDC) recipients only, and normally these recipients are referred to this office as job applicants by personnel of the Department of Social Services and Housing.

The other four Oahu offices, as well as neighbor island offices, offer direct job referrals, job development, employment hints and information, information on training programs and apprenticeships, testing, and job counseling. They also provide special services to veterans, solicit jobs, and make employer contacts. When requested, the Honolulu Office periodically tests, screens and refers applicants for apprenticeships with the various unions.

In addition, the Hawaii State Employment Service offices make available to their registered clientele daily computerized listings of available jobs from the State Job Bank. From this extensive list, job seekers can select for themselves jobs for which they qualify.

The types of jobs listed with the Employment Offices are full-time, part-time and temporary jobs. Jobs are listed from private industry and government, and range from blue collar to white collar. They include jobs in driving, trade, maintenance, sales, food service, sewing, domestic, clerical, accounting, laundry and others. Technical as well as personnel and managerial positions are also listed. Depending on the labor market condition, the availability of certain types of jobs will vary and will be limited. (See Appendix A, page 171, for data on applicants served and placements made.)

Six other offices of the Hawaii State Employment Service are located on the neighbor islands of Hawaii, Maui, Kauai and Molokai. The addresses of these offices as well as those of the Oahu offices, are as follows:

Island of Hawaii
Hilo Office
180 Kinoole Street
Hilo, Hawaii 96720

Kona Office
Post Office Building
Kealakekua, Hawaii 96750

The Island of Maui

Wailuku Office
2180 Main Street
Wailuku, Maui 96793

Lahaina Office
840 Wainee Street
Lahaina, Maui 96761

Island of Kauai

Kauai Office
3016 Umi Street, Room 204
Lihue, Kauai 96766

Island of Molokai

Kaunakakai Office
Ala Malama Street
Kaunakakai, Hawaii 96748

Island of Oahu

Honolulu Office
1040 South King Street, Second Floor
Honolulu, Hawaii 96814

Waipahu Office
Waipahu Shopping Village
94-226 Leoku Street
Waipahu, Hawaii 96797

Kaneohe Office
45-1144 Kamehameha Highway
(near Kahuhipa Street)
Kaneohe, Hawaii 96744

Kalihi Office
401 Waiakamilo Road
Honolulu, Hawaii 96817

WIN Office*
715 South King Street, 2nd Floor
Honolulu, Hawaii 96813
*Services AFDC recipients only.

U.S. CIVIL SERVICE COMMISSION

The Federal Job Information Center, a part of the U.S. Civil Service Commission, publicizes jobs, recruits, tests and selects job applicants for Federal Civil Service positions* in Hawaii, Guam and the Pacific Overseas Area (which includes Korea, Okinawa, Japan, Philippines, Taiwan, Midway, American Samoa, and Trust Territories)[1]

*Except for the Postal Service.

The U.S. Civil Service Commission does not conduct competitive examinations or refer job applicants for postal positions in Hawaii or Guam.[2] The application and examination functions are performed by the U.S.Postal Service. The contact point is the Postmaster of the Post Office where employment is sought.[3]

As a job seeker, you should be prepared to take proficiency, aptitude and other tests, as well as be prepared to furnish required documents such as licenses, certificates, degrees, work experience summaries, service records and other documents. Certified and current typing and shorthand proficiency certificates can be submitted.

To be considered for a Federal job in Hawaii, the job applicant must (1) meet the specific job position qualifications and requirements, (2) be a United States Citizen or an American National and (3) normally furnish proof of established residence in Hawaii. Anyone with an Alien or Refugee status is not entitled to apply.

As an applicant, you should check out the requirements for each job applied for.

The numerous departments, agencies, commissions and offices of the Federal service are required to conduct periodic recruitment and selection due to personnel turnover, changing needs, and other factors. Information in the Oahu Telephone Directory, under the United States Government section, will provide you with some idea of the various Federal agencies, commissions, and offices which operate here in Hawaii. This Directory will also give some indication of the types of occupations which are utilized for operational needs.

As to the number of applicants and hires, during the fiscal year 1975-1976, the total hires for Hawaii and the Pacific Overseas Area numbered about 1,200; of this number, about 600, or one-half were blue collar workers, about one-fourth were clerical workers, and about one-fourth were various other types of managerial. technical, and administrative personnel.[4] However, about 21,000 applications were processed.[5] The U.S. Civil Service Commission also has a successful recruitment program for various apprenticeships.

Examples of current types of exams available through the Honolulu Federal Job Information Center are as follows:[6]

Professional and Administrative Careers (PACE)
Lower Professional and Administrative Careers (PACE)
Educational positions
Army Reserve Technicians
Various other Professional, Technical and Administrative positions
Engineering and Architectural
Physical Sciences
Computer Services
Law Enforcement
Health Services
Life Sciences
Maintenance and Service Workers
Worker Trainee jobs
Various other blue collar type jobs as mechanical, trades, equipment operators and others.

Under each of these categories of occupational groupings, many individual types of jobs are listed. You should be aware that specific types of jobs will only be open for recruitment depending on agency needs, expansions, and other factors.

The address of the Federal Job Information Center is:

Federal Job Information Center
Honolulu Area Office
New Federal Building
(Prince Kalanianaole Federal Building)
300 Ala Moana Boulevard
Honolulu, Hawaii 96813

HAWAII STATE DEPARTMENT OF PERSONNEL SERVICES

The Hawaii State Department of Personnel Services publicizes jobs and recruits, tests and selects job applicants for seventeen state government departments, including the Office of Governor, the Judicial, and the Legislative Branches.[7]

The basic requirements for job consideration, other than meeting the specific job position requirements and qualifications, are that, "applicants must be citizens, permanent resident Aliens or Nationals of the United States and residents of Hawaii. . . ."[8] A new one-year residency requirement has been legislated and job seekers must meet this requirement in order to apply for jobs with the State government.

Until decided otherwise, applicants with "Refugee Status" who have their I-94 Arrival and Departure Record certificates stamped "Employment Authorized" by the Federal Immigration and Naturalization Service can apply with this State Personnel Service Department for positions provided that all individual job qualifications, residency and other requirements for jobs applied for are met.

As with other civil service procedures, you should be prepared to take aptitude, proficiency and other tests, as well as be prepared to furnish the required documents, such as licenses, certificates, degrees, work experience and service records. Certified and current typing and shorthand certificates can be submitted.

The following data will give you an idea of the volume of applicants who apply with this state agency. During the fiscal year of 1974 to 1975, there were 1,771 job vacancies[9] filled by competitive examinations, and these included permanent full-time hires as well as temporary and part-time positions.

However, of 18,735 applicants who were screened, 13,840 were accepted as meeting the minimum qualifications of the positions applied for.[10] Applicants who were rejected for one reason or another numbered 4,895.[11]

During the 1975 to 1976 fiscal year, there were 2,623 job vacancies filled by competitive examinations, and these included permanent full-time hires as well as temporary and part-time positions.[12] However, 26,708 applicants were screened, and 19,309 were accepted as meeting the minimum qualifications of the positions applied for.[13] Applicants who were rejected for one reason or another numbered 7,399.[14]

During the 1974-1975 fiscal year, there were 18,311 applications received by this agency,[15] and in the 1975 to 1976 period, this same agency received a total of 31,021 job applications.[16]

The seventeen State Departments of government for which Civil Service positions are recruited, including other offices, are as follows:[17]

Departments of
- Accounting and General Services
- Agriculture
- Attorney General
- Budget and Finance
- Defense
- Education
- Hawaiian Home Lands
- Health
- Labor and Industrial Relations
- Land and Natural Resources
- Personnel Services
- Planning and Economic Development
- Regulatory Agencies
- Social Services and Housing
- Taxation
- Transportation
- University of Hawaii

Governor's Office

Lieutenant Governor's Office
Judiciary
Legislative Reference Bureau

The State Department of Personnel Services is located at:

Department of Personnel Services
State of Hawaii
825 Mililani Street, Room 402
Honolulu, Hawaii 96813

COUNTY CIVIL SERVICE DEPARTMENTS

The Honolulu City and County Department of Civil Service publicizes jobs and recruits, tests and selects job applicants for the nineteen departments of this county.[18]

The basic civil service requirements, other than meeting the specific job position requirements, are that job seekers be United States Citizens, Permanent Alien Residents, or American Nationals, meet a one-year residency requirement, and be under 70 years of age.* While "Refugees" do not fall within the meaning of Citizens or Permanent Aliens, this class of people with official Refugee Status, until decided otherwise, is permitted to seek employment with the Honolulu County, provided that all individual job qualifications, residency and other requirements for job applied for are met.

As a job seeker, you should be prepared to submit certificates, licenses, degrees and other documentary requirements, as well as be prepared to take physical and/or written proficiency, aptitude and other tests for civil service positions. Certified and current typing and shorthand proficiency certificates can be submitted.

The Honolulu City and County civil service jobs are comprised of ten occupational groupings and 292 occupational classes.[19] With these classes, a myriad of jobs emerge which function to service the various departments and offices.

Direct consultation with personnel of the Honolulu City and County Civil Service Department is recommended for more

*By Hawaii State Law, 70 is the mandatory age of retirement.

detailed descriptions of specific occupations. However, you can be aware of the types of positions periodically available within the Honolulu County civil service jobs by the following ten occupational groupings:[20]

Clerical and Allied Occupations
Public Administration and Allied Occupations
Recreational Occupations
Biological and Physical Science Occupations
Engineering and Allied Occupations
Medical and Allied Occupations
Public Protection, Inspection and Investigation Occupations
Labor, Custodial and Domestic Occupations
Trades and Crafts
Mechanical Equipment Operators

During the fiscal year of July 1975 to June 1976, the Honolulu County hired 455 new full-time civil service employees.[21] During this period, there were actually 4,993 new hires, including the same new full-time hires, though most of the hires were in such categories as part-time, temporary, contractual, summer hires, CETA,* moves from one program to another, and others.[22]

* Concentrated Employment Training Act

During this same period, there was an average of 166 job applicants per job, and 15,630 job applicants were screened by personnel of the Honolulu County Department of Civil Service.[23] In the previous fiscal year, July 1974 to June 1975, there was an average of 95 job applicants competing for each job, and 15,908 job applicants were screened by civil service personnel.[24]

The civil service departments of the other three Neighbor Island counties autonomously perform functions similar to those of the Honolulu County Department of Civil Service. The basic requirements for job consideration in these counties, other than meeting specific job requirements, are similar to those of the Honolulu County Department of Civil Service.

Following are the addresses of the four county civil service departments:

Department of Civil Service
City and County of Honolulu
City Hall Annex
Honolulu, Hawaii 96813

Department of Personnel Services
County of Hawaii
25 Aupuni Street
Hilo, Hawaii 96720

Department of Personnel Services
County of Kauai
4280 Rice Street
Lihue, Hawaii 96766

Department of Personnel Services
County of Maui
200 South High Street
Wailuku, Hawaii 96793

For occupational information purposes, various departments and offices of the Honolulu City and County are listed as follows:[25]

- Departments
    - Auditoriums
    - Board of Water Supply (semi-autonomous)
    - Budget
    - Building
    - Civil Service
    - Corporation Counsel
    - Data Systems
    - Finance
    - Fire Department
    - General Planning
    - Health
    - Housing and Community Development
    - Land Utilization

Medical Examiner
Parks and Recreation
Police
Prosecuting Attorney
Public Works
Transportation Services

Other Offices
Civil Defense Agency
Managing Director's Office
Municipal Reference and Records Center
Neighborhood Commission
Office of Human Resources
Office of Information and Complaint
Honolulu Police Commission
Royal Hawaiian Band
And various commissions, committees, council services and the City Clerk's Office

HAWAII STATE DEPARTMENT OF EDUCATION

The Hawaii State Department of Education is the agency which recruits, ascertains the qualifications of, and selects teachers and other professional staff for the public schools in Hawaii. These are non-civil service positions. The grade levels are from kindergarten to the twelfth grades, and schools encompassing these grade levels are dispersed throughout the State.

Teachers are generally recruited as elementary or secondary school teachers. Personnel for other professional, but non-administrative, positions are also recruited.

Applications for employment as professionals, other than civil service positions, are made directly to the main office. As with applications for other professional positions, the job seeker should be prepared to submit the necessary copies of degrees, certifications, and other documents. However, job seekers should be aware of a recent one-year residency requirement which must be met in order to submit job applications with the Department of Education.

The addresses and locations of the main personnel office and other district offices of the Department of Education are as follows:

Main Office
Personnel Office
Department of Education
State of Hawaii
Liliuokalani Building
1390 Miller Street, 3rd Floor
Honolulu, Hawaii 96813

District Offices on Oahu
Central Oahu District Office
1136 California Avenue
Wahiawa, Hawaii 96786

Honolulu District Office
4945 Kilauea Avenue
Honolulu, Hawaii 96816

Leeward District Office
94-366 Pupupani Street
Waipahu, Hawaii 96797

Windward Oahu District Office
45-955 Kamehameha Highway
Kaneohe, Hawaii 96744

District Office on Hawaii
Hawaii District Office
75 Aupuni Street
Hilo, Hawaii 96720

District Office on Kauai
Kauai District Office
3060 Eiwa Street
State Office Building
Lihue, Hawaii 96766

District Office on Maui
Maui District Office
54 High Street
Wailuku, Hawaii 96793

HUMAN SERVICE CENTERS

Currently, there are six Human Service Centers on Oahu. Job referral is one of the services offered by these centers. They also have the daily computerized listings of available jobs from the State Job Bank, and they should provide job referral and job information services to people residing within established districts.

The addresses and locations of these centers are as follows:

Kalihi-Palama Human Service Center
(across Farrington High School in the Kam Housing)
1440 Alokele Street
Honolulu, Hawaii 96817

Nanakuli Human Service Center
(at Nanaikapono Elementary School)
89-195 Farrington Highway
Nanakuli, Hawaii 96792

Waimanalo Human Service Center
(across Waimanalo Elementary School)
41-1347 Kalanianaole Highway
Waimanalo, Hawaii 96795

Maile Human Service Center
(at Maile Elementary School)
87-360 Kulaaupuni Street
Maile, Hawaii 96792

Waianae Human Service Center
(at Waianae Elementary School)
85-220 McArthur Street
Waianae, Hawaii 96792

Makaha Human Service Center
(at Waianae Elementary School)
85-220 McArthur Street
Waianae, Hawaii 96792

HONOLULU CITY AND COUNTY *CETA* CENTERS

The City and County of Honolulu administers, and is responsible for, two referral and training programs: The Honolulu Job Resource Center and the Waianae CETA Center.

While CETA on-the-job training and other services are emphasized, personnel of these centers do make job referrals for their registered clientele from job listings which are solicited or called in.

The addresses and locations of these CETA Centers are:

Honolulu Job Resource Center
(on Pier 11)
79 South Nimitz Highway
Honolulu, Hawaii 96813

Waianae CETA Center
(in Waianae Satellite
City Hall, Room 7)
85-670 Farrington Highway
Waianae, Hawaii 96792

AGENCY AND INSTITUTIONAL SOURCES WHICH GIVE INDIRECT JOB REFERRALS OR INFORMATION

VETERANS ADMINISTRATION

The Veterans Administration provides many services to veterans. While the administration is not a job placement agency, counselors and personnel do make referrals to placement agencies, provide job information, and explain veterans' reemployment rights.

The Veterans Administration is located at:

Veterans Administration
New Federal Building
(Prince Kalanianaole Federal Building)
300 Ala Moana Boulevard
Honolulu, Hawaii 96813

HAWAII STATE DIVISION OF VOCATIONAL REHABILITATION

The Division of Vocational Rehabilitation counsels and services people with disabilities and impairments which are sufficiently severe so as to affect their health, lives and livelihood. Some job development for these persons is performed. The personnel of this division have established working relationships with personnel of the State Employment Service through which clientele referrals are made to the employment service for job placement. Some personnel of this division also establish contacts with employers and should be able to provide basic job information to people they serve.

The following is a list of some Vocational Rehabilitation offices throughout the State:

Island of Oahu

Main State Office
Division of Vocational Rehabilitation
Dept. of Social Services
State of Hawaii
1390 Miller Street
Honolulu, Hawaii 96813

Oahu Branch
Division of Vocational Rehabilitation
Dept. of Social Services
State of Hawaii
1390 Miller Street
Honolulu, Hawaii 96813

Island of Hawaii

Hilo Branch
Division of Vocational Rehabilitation
Dept. of Social Services
State of Hawaii
75 Aupuni Street
Hilo, Hawaii 96720

Kona Branch
Division of Vocational Rehabilitation
Dept. of Social Services
State of Hawaii
P. O. Box 127
Kealakekua, Hawaii 96750

Island of Kauai

Kauai Branch
Division of Vocational Rehabilitation
Dept. of Social Services
State of Hawaii
3060 Eiwa Street
Lihue, Hawaii 96766

Island of Maui

Maui Branch
Division of Vocational Rehabilitation
Dept. of Social Services
State of Hawaii
54 South High Street
Wailuku, Maui 96793

HAWAII STATE DEPARTMENT OF SOCIAL SERVICES AND HOUSING

This State Department is not a job placement agency, but AFDC recipients are referred to the State Employment WIN

Office for job placement by personnel of this agency. Other clientele of this agency are also referred to the State Employment Service for job placement services. Personnel of this agency, while not directly involved with job placement, should be able to provide basic information about state placement services.

Five branch offices and numerous units providing services are spread throughout the State, but the addresses and locations of the main office on Oahu and neighbor island branches of this department are as follows:

Main State Office
Department of Social Services and Housing
State of Hawaii
Liliuokalani Building
1390 Miller Street, 2nd Floor
Honolulu, Hawaii 96813

Island of Hawaii
Hawaii Branch, Department of Social Services and Housing
State of Hawaii
75 Aupuni Street
Hilo, Hawaii 96720

Island of Maui
Maui Branch, Department of Social Services and Housing
State of Hawaii
State Office Building
Main Street
Wailuku, Hawaii 96793

Island of Kauai
Kauai Branch, Department of Social Services and Housing
State of Hawaii
State Office Building
3060 Eiwa Street
Lihue, Hawaii 96766

Island of Molokai

Molokai Branch, Department of Social Services and Housing
State of Hawaii
P. O. Box 7
Kaunakakai, Hawaii 96748

STATE IMMIGRANT CENTERS

Immigrant service centers were established by Act 299, the Progressive Neighborhood Act, to assist new immigrants arriving after 1965 to adjust to, and be acculturated into, the communities. While other health and orientation problems are on-going concerns, these service centers are primarily concerned with the job and housing problems of immigrants and therefore provide job referrals to the proper placement agencies. The goal of these service centers is to help immigrants become self-sufficient.

Immigrant service centers are located at the following addresses:

Kalihi-Palama Immigrant Service Center
904 Kohou Street, Room 201
Honolulu, Hawaii 96817

Leeward Y.W.C.A. and Immigrant Services
(Westgate Shopping Center)
94-366 Pupupani Street, Room 201
Waipahu, Hawaii 96797

Cosmopolitan Social Services
(Kalihi Union Church)
2214 North King Street
Honolulu, Hawaii 96819

Susanna Wesley Community Center
1117 Kaili Street
Honolulu, Hawaii 96819

Maryknoll Sisters
1035 North School Street
Honolulu, Hawaii 96817

JOB SOURCES, PRINTED AND PUBLICIZED, WHICH PROVIDE JOB LEADS AND INFORMATION

NEWSPAPER HELP WANTED ADS

An important source of job information is the help wanted classified ads in the two major newspapers. An examination of the wanted sections will reveal advertisments placed by various sources, such as private business, government agencies, organizarions, individuals, and private employment agencies. The State and Honolulu County Civil Service Departments also periodically advertise job openings in the local newspapers.

Not to be neglected as a job source are the ads in the newspapers printed by the various community, ethnic and special interest groups. More than twenty-five of these are listed in the yellow pages of the Oahu Telephone Directory.[26]

One of the reasons employers advertise through want ads is that they want fast responses from applicants. The reader should note that "answering advertisements in newspapers" was one of the three top ranking methods used by job seekers who were interviewed in a U.S. Department of Labor survey. (See Chapter 4 for further information)

PRINTED AND CIRCULATED FLYERS AND MATERIALS, INCLUDING OCCUPATIONAL, PROFESSIONAL, ASSOCIATION JOURNALS AND OTHER PUBLICATIONS

Civil service agencies distribute notices of job vacancies and job information to governmental agencies, educational institutions – public and private, special interest groups, and non-profit organizations.

The numerous nationally and state-distributed occupational, professional and association journals, publications and newsletters often advertise professional job openings;

however, Hawaii tends to have a limited number of openings listed. These publications can be found in locations such as personnel offices, colleges, business offices and libraries.

The community colleges and other University of Hawaii campuses also advertise job openings in their monthly bulletins and in the Manoa Campus Bulletin.* The community college and Manoa Campus bulletins are available to the faculty and staff of the University of Hawaii system.

While job openings are not listed in the Hawaii Career Directory, it is an informative publication, published annually by the Manoa Campus Placement and Career Planning Office. This directory lists a host of businesses, industries and institutional job sources for college and university students.[27]

Community associations and other special interest groups periodically distribute flyers and worthy news items which may publicize ads on employment needs.

In addition, notices on bulletin boards located in various shopping centers and community centers, at times, advertise some job openings.

YELLOW PAGES OF THE OAHU TELEPHONE DIRECTORY

The yellow pages of the Oahu Telephone Directory provide a wealth of information about industries and types of businesses which operate on Oahu. Neighbor Island telephone directories also provide similar information. The names of the companies and businesses, and their advertisements, will give some indication of type of jobs needed to operate the businesses, as well as the locations of these firms. This information is useful in making inquiries about and applying for jobs. For example, the names and locations of the unions on Oahu are listed alphabetically under "Labor Organizations". The AFL-CIO unions are also listed in the front of the telephone directory under the "A" section. The Telephone directory is readily available in Hawaii and should also be found in most city libraries on the mainland.

---

* A weekly publication of the University of Hawaii, at Manoa, during semesters.

PERSONNEL OFFICES OF AGENCIES, INSTITUTIONS, PRIVATE FIRMS, UNIONS, SMALL BUSINESS ESTABLISHMENTS, THE MILITARY AND PRIVATE EMPLOYMENT AGENCIES WHICH OFFER JOBS

PERSONNEL OFFICES OF FEDERAL AGENCIES AND MILITARY BASES

While the recruitment and selection of Federal Civil Service jobs are centralized through the Federal Job Information Center, there also exist personnel offices for various Federal agencies and military bases, such as the Pearl Harbor Naval Shipyard, Hickam Air Force Base, Camp Smith, Schofield, Fort Shafter, and Fort DeRussy. These organizations periodically hire non-civil service personnel through the use of non-appropriated funds.

In addition, the Non-Commissioned Officers Clubs and Officers Clubs, which are situated within these bases and which provide food and refreshments, should not be overlooked as job sources.

The Pacific Regional Exchange (PACEX) and the Hawaii Regional Exchange are not true governmental agencies. These agencies handle the post exchanges on the Army and Air Force bases, here and elsewhere in the Pacific. Job vacancies, when they do occur, range from blue collar to white collar jobs, from maintenance and clerical to technical and supervisory/managerial positions, including positions for food services. Personnel in the higher level positions within PACEX are expected to travel.

Pacific Exchange System Headquarters
919 Ala Moana Boulevard
(near Ward Avenue)
Honolulu, Hawaii 96814

Hawaii Regional Exchange
919 Ala Moana Boulevard
(near Ward Avenue)
Honolulu, Hawaii 96814

STATE COMMUNITY COLLEGES AND UNIVERSITY OF HAWAII CAMPUSES

There are nine campuses within the University of Hawaii system. Of these nine, three are four-year institutions and six are two-year colleges. The Manoa Campus and West Oahu College, both four-year institutions, and four two-year colleges — Leeward Community College, Kapiolani Community College, Honolulu Community College and Windward Community College — are all situated on Oahu. Maui Community College and Kauai Community College, both two-year colleges, are both situated on their respective islands. Hawaii Community College, a two-year college, has been incorporated as part of Hilo College, a four-year institution. Both are situated on the island of Hawaii.

Except for civil service positions, the recruitment and selection of faculty, research, technical student services personnel, support and administrative positions are decentralized; that is, in principle each campus is empowered to recruit and select such personnel. These positions are non-civil service. To determine which jobs are civil service or non-civil service positions, the job seeker should check with the campus personnel offices or with the State Department of Personnel Services.

Letters of inquiry and applications for employment can be made directly to each of the campuses. The job seeker should be prepared to submit letters of reference, degrees, documented achievements, resumes and other documents, as well as be prepared to face campus personnel screening committees.

The one-year residency requirement does not apply to certain personnel recruited by the University of Hawaii; however, all persons recruited as Administrative/Professional/ Technical personnel are subject to the residency requirement.*

* Job seekers should check with the personnel offices of the various University of Hawaii campuses to ascertain more specifically which positions are exempt from the one-year requirement.

Students enrolled in these institutions can seek out job leads and information from their campus placement offices or from other offices on their campus which have been designated to assist students in these areas.

Following is a list of addresses and locations of the major public two-year colleges and four-year institutions in Hawaii:

Two-Year Colleges

Leeward Community College
96-045 Ala Ike
Pearl City, Hawaii 96782

Kapiolani Community College
620 Pensacola Street
Honolulu, Hawaii 96814

Honolulu Community College
874 Dillingham Boulevard
Honolulu, Hawaii 96817

Maui Community College
310 Kaahumanu Avenue
Kahului, Hawaii 96732

Kauai Community College
RR 1, Box 216
Lihue, Hawaii 96766

Hawaii Community College
1175 Manono Street
Hilo, Hawaii 96720

Four-Year Institutions

University of Hawaii at Manoa
2444 Dole Street
Honolulu, Hawaii 96822

West Oahu College
(Niu Town Square Bldg., 2nd Floor)
98-1247 Kaahumanu Street
Aiea, Hawaii 96701

Hilo College
333 West Lanikaula Street
Hilo, Hawaii 96720

PRIVATE SCHOOLS, COLLEGES, BUSINESS COLLEGES, AND DAY CARE CENTERS

As with the public educational institutions, the private educational schools and colleges are comprised of various grade levels and programs, from day care centers to grade schools to business and technical schools to the college level.

Under "Schools" in the yellow pages of the Oahu Telephone Directory, the various types of instructional specialties comprise about 6½ pages and include public and private schools and colleges. For example, about 179 Day Care centers on Oahu cater to pre-kindergarten youngsters up to the grade school level.[28] The operational staffing needs of these centers and other private schools range from maintenance to teaching support personnel to administrative personnel. While salaries generally are not comparable to those of the public educational system, these institutions are sources for jobs.

The job applicant requirements for employment in private schools vary with each institution.

PRIVATE NON-PROFIT INSTITUTIONS

Most private non-profit institutions and agencies are supported through contributions and other types of funding and exist to provide special services to people. Hawaii's Aloha United Way, for example, helps to fund 56 agencies which deal with human service programs. Such agencies, though small in staffing, utilize personnel who assist people.

Aloha United Way
200 North Vineyard Blvd., 7th floor
Honolulu, Hawaii 96817

PERSONNEL OFFICES OF PRIVATE FIRMS AND SMALL ESTABLISHMENTS

The personnel offices of private firms are very good sources for job searching. While the following figures provide only partial data, the job seeker can gain an understanding of the numbers and types of businesses which are licensed to operate in Hawaii. During the 1976 calendar year, 105,904 State General Excise Licenses were issued.[29] The types of licensed businesses are not broken down into categories, but according to data based on the 1975-1976 fiscal year tax returns, there are at least 11,442 business corporations, 5,382 business partnerships, 1,042 small business corporations, and 5,057 fiduciaries operating in Hawaii.[30] In 1973, sole proprietorships numbered 33,143.[31]

Most of the larger firms retain personnel interviewers who screen and process job applicants for all of their various branches and outlets. As an example, most banks have centralized interviewing and processing procedures through which personnel of the main branches usually interview and process job applicants for all of their branches.

In many of the smaller establishments, interviewing and hiring of job applicants is done by the owner, through the manager, or some key personnel.

Private industry will "reach out" for job applicants through advertisements, listings with public and private employment agencies, and other means, but you, as a job seeker should also seek out employers. There are shopping centers, service stations, super markets, restaurants, banks, insurance companies, department stores, gift shops, hotels, trucking firms, hospitals, and many more businesses.

Walk down the street in any district where these businesses operate and you can familiarize yourself with, inquire, and submit applications to these establishments.

The U.S. Department of Labor survey pointed out that "direct application was named by the largest proportions of workers as the method by which they found their present jobs." (See Chapter 4 for further information)

UNIONS

The trade labor unions, particularly those which are involved in construction, in principle and practice, make referrals directly for members, and occasionally for others, through their offices. The Building and Construction Trade unions generally have Union Shop Agreements with employers.

Currently, members of trade unions who are on waiting lists with their locals for jobs are given first preference.

Other unions, such as the maritime unions, function in the same capacity in servicing their members, but shipping-out is tight. There is a surplus of unionized seamen.

The unions which represent the hotel industry also, in principle and in practice, make direct referrals for members to job openings with business establishments which they represent. When the need arises, non-members are also referred.

As mentioned previously, the names and locations of unions on Oahu can be found in the Oahu Telephone Directory.

PRIVATE EMPLOYMENT AGENCIES

Currently, there are close to fifty private employment agencies on Oahu.[32] These private employment agencies solicit jobs and refer applicants to job openings, most generally *for a fee* based on commission schedules established by law. These private agencies, unlike state agencies, operate on a profit basis. According to advertisements, there appears to be only one private agency on Oahu which does not charge fees to job seekers.

According to the telephone directories of the neighbor islands, one private agency is listed for the Island of Hawaii, two for Maui and one for Kauai.

HAWAII OFFICE OF ECONOMIC OPPORTUNITY

The Hawaii Office of Economic Opportunity coordinates community action programs throughout the State which help to meet the needs and priorities of residents with low incomes.

The Honolulu Community Action Program (HCAP) through five of its district offices on Oahu, provides human services projects for low income families throughout Oahu, and service clientele according to residence in census tract districts.[33] On Oahu, there are about 250 employees engaged in administrative, teaching, para-professional, outreach, nursing, maintenance, food services, driving and clerical work.[34]

The following projects are among the endeavors which HCAP covers, and these include:[35]

Transportation services project
Headstart project for pre-school children
Youth awareness project
Alternative school project - working with drop-outs
Home-maker services project - aid to the elderly
Foodstamp outreach project
Nutrition and socialization project - an elderly
stimulation project
Agricultural gardening project

Other community action offices are situated on the Neighbor Islands and provide similar services.

Job seekers should be aware of a possible one-year residency requirement in order to apply for jobs with state offices which administer and carry out these programs.

State Office
Hawaii Office of Economic Opportunity
904 Kohou Street
Honolulu, Hawaii 96817

Oahu Offices
Honolulu Community Action Program, Inc.
Main Office
838 South Beretania Street, Suite 202
Honolulu, Hawaii 96813

Waianae-Nanakuli District Office
85-555 Farrington Highway
P. O. Box 974
Waianae, Hawaii 96792

Central District Office
99-102 Kalaloa Street
Aiea, Hawaii 96701

Kalihi-Palama District Office
1545-107B Linapuni Street
Honolulu, Hawaii 96819

Windward District Office
45-252 Waikalua Road
P.O. Box 792
Kaneohe, Hawaii 96744

Leahi District Office
1915 Palolo Avenue
Honolulu, Hawaii 96816

Hawaii County Office
Hawaii County Economic Opportunity Council
46 Keawe Street
Hilo, Hawaii 96720

Kauai County Office
Economic Opportunity, Inc.
P. O. Box 1027
(Wehe Street)
Lihue, Hawaii 96766

Maui County Office
Economic Opportunity, Inc.
189 Kaahumanu Avenue
Kahului, Hawaii 96732

PROFESSIONAL ASSOCIATIONS, COMMUNITY ASSOCIATIONS, CHURCH GROUPS, CLUBS, FRATERNAL ORGANIZATIONS, AND OTHER SOURCES WHICH PROVIDE JOB LEADS AND INFLUENCE

Another method of finding assistance in job seeking is to ask fellow members of associations, clubs, fraternal groups, fraternities, sororities, cultural groups, or social, business or church groups to which you belong. The comradeship, friendship, or other relationships established by belonging can provide avenues to information, job leads, and personal influences for you as a job seeker.

PEOPLE WHO PROVIDE JOB LEADS, INFORMATION AND INFLUENCE

A valuable, if not primary, resource for assistance is family, relatives and friends, especially if you as a job seeker encounter difficulties in your job search.

Pride and a sense of independence or, possibly alienation, may prevent you from turning to these people, but whatever the situation, make use of these sources. Be drawn to them. It is possible when these sources are sought out, political and personal influences will be exerted in your behalf.

Politicians, political party members, public officials, company officials, organizational and institutional personnel, union officials, administrators, managers, and supervisors whom you or others close to you know, should be contacted for assistance in seeking jobs - especially when higher level or prime jobs are being sought. Other viable sources for assistance in finding jobs would be members of professional, community, cultural and other organizations to which you belong.

Placement personnel, vocational counselors, personnel officers, business teachers, and those whose jobs require them to keep abreast of the employment situation should also be sought out for job leads and information.

KEY FACTORS TO REMEMBER

Numerous resources exist to assist the job seeker. While access to some resources may be more difficult, many of these resources are easily accessible, but they have to be sought out.

First, plan your job source contacts or leads. Then seek out and file applications consistently with all available sources until a job is found. And when a job is obtained and is not quite satisfactory, keep looking for a more suitable job. In the meantime, however, retain the job that you have if you are employed. Remember, searching for a job may most likely not be an easy task for you, and thus, should not be a crisis situation. It should be planned. A haphazard and unplanned approach may work at times, but a planned approach will be more effective.

Common sense, sincerity, a positive attitude, persistence, and an understanding of the realities of labor market conditions and of job seeking should dictate the course of action you take. The results depend on your efforts.

Seeking out these resources and applying for jobs may not be an easy task and experience for you, but keep applying for jobs consistently and on a regular basis. Look upon job searching as working for yourself - as an investment in yourself. Minimize your personal problems and recreational activities, if possible, and concentrate on getting a job. If one prospective employer does not come through, keep your spirits up and contact as many resources and employers as possible. The time and energy that you invest will eventually pay off! Perhaps not in a desired job, but a job nonetheless!

CHAPTER 2

OVERVIEW OF LABOR MARKET INFORMATION

Labor market data provides the job seeker with basic labor and occupational information about the community and industries in which jobs are located. This chapter will focus upon employers' expectations, leading industries, existing industries, job trends, availability of jobs, prevailing pay rates, unions, work force, unemployment rates, turnover factors, and other information to aid in job searching.

OVERVIEW OF EMPLOYERS

As in any free enterprise system, employers are understandably in private business to make a profit. Therefore, whether a firm has only one employee or thousands, you can reasonably expect that the employer will want the "best," and preferably the most productive employee; or employees who are responsible, reliable, honest and capable and who possess desirable personal and work characteristics.

Ask yourself, if you were an employer, what type of employees would you hire for your business? As a typical business man or woman, what qualities would you desire in an employee? What are the employer expectations which have a bearing on job seeking? Put yourself into the employer's position. What do employers look for when they fill a position vacancy? What are the kinds of things which turn off employers? What turns them on? What are the tangibles and the intangibles? Simply speaking, the tangibles are what employers can read about you, see of you, and personally hear from you. In other words, what you say, what you wear, what you write about yourself will affect employers. Examples of tangibles are your work experiences, personal history, appearance, resume, applications and references.

The intangibles are what the employers feel or intuitively sense about you. They are how employers react to you as a person. How you speak, how you behave, and how you react will have an effect on the employer. Examples of intangibles are your tone of voice, your posture, your facial expressions, your personal mannerisms, your ability to look directly at the interviewer, your reaction to questions, your personality projection, your sense of responsibility and your lifestyle values.

Whatever the methods of approach utilized, impressions made, or influences exerted by job seekers, the employers still want the best and most productive employees for the salaries they are willing to pay. A fact to be remembered is that in the final analysis, it is the employers who hire.

The following will provide you with some idea about how employers feel and what qualities they are looking for in potential employees.

SURVEYS

Sample Survey on Oahu:

The purposes of a random survey conducted by the author a few years ago of some employers on Oahu, Hawaii, were to obtain data on what qualities the employers were looking for in two-year college graduates and students as potential employees and to disseminate such information to students and others. The Oahu employers surveyed were from such businesses as department stores, finance companies, banks, service stations, computer firms, restaurants, drive-ins, government agencies, retail stores, insurance companies, and others.

This sample survey on Oahu asked three questions of employers. Approximately 300 questionnaires were mailed and 47 responded. The questions and responses from the first mailing were as follows:

Question No. 1

What things do you consider most important in job interviews that students should learn or be aware of?

The forty-seven employers responded in order of importance:

Appearance
Experience
Knowledge
Honesty
Personality and Ability to get along with others
Alertness - Attentiveness
Motivation - Purpose
Ability to converse well and good English usage
Preparedness for interviews
Self Confidence
Resume and Academic background
Positive Attitude - Enthusiasm
Oral and Physical expression
Promptness
Application filling - neat and complete
Aptitudes
Reasons for leaving
Education
Response to questions
Desirability
Length of time employed by one company
Minimum salary acceptable
Practicality
Conciseness and to the point
Ability to follow instructions
Hours
Applicant's questions about company
Hearing

As the job seeker will note, seven of the first ten "order of importance" responses were "intangibles."

Question No. 2

Aside from training, education and work experience what other things do you look for in an interview with junior college graduates and students?

The employers responded in order of importance:

Personality
Appearance
Attitude
Alertness
Educational (achievements)
Future Goal
Physical (condition)
Self Confidence
Personal Stability
Honesty
Sincerity in people
Ambition
Position
Responsibility

Again, as with responses to question number 1, about ten of the fourteen "order of importance" responses were also intangibles.

Question No. 3

Will awareness and application of these considerations help graduates and students achieve employment with your company?

Forty-seven employers responded "Yes" to this question, and none answered "No."

A Thought to Consider

As a job seeker, you should consider the employer's emphasis on intangibles as desired qualities of potential employees, and if needed, strive for self-improvement.

A Mainland Survey

A survey was conducted on the Mainland a few years ago by the Western College Placement Association to determine employers' attitudes regarding applicant characteristics, academic preparation, extracurricular experiences, and interview behavior in selecting college graduates for employment.[1] This survey resulted in responses from 101 companies from 17 industrial groupings on the Mainland.[2] Brought to light in this survey were employers' responses on critical factors, some of which are listed as follows:

EMPLOYER ATTITUDE SURVEY ITEMS[3]

A. Academic Characteristics of Applicant

1. Student's Major
2. Type of College from which Applicant Graduated (Four Year Bachelor Degree)
3. Student's Academic Performance

B. Academic Electives, Honors, Experience

1. Student's Academic Activities
2. Undergraduate Options
3. Work Experience
4. Extracurricular activities

C. Non-Academic and Permanent Personal Characteristics

1. Past Record
2. Student's Military Status
3. Personal Characteristics
4. Applicant's Lifestyle

D. Applicant Interview Behavior and Related Information

1. Appearance
2. Group Affiliations
3. Interview Behavior
    a. General
    b. Eye Contact
    c. Handshake

4. The Applicant's Expectations about Employment
5. Timing of Interview Questions
6. The Applicant's Mood or Attitude in the Interview
7. Miscellaneous Questions

As an example of the employers' attitude, one of the items under survey, "the applicant's mood or attitude during the interview", was evaluated by the interviewer on the basis of whether the applicant was:[4]

assertive	grateful	nervous or tense
composed	independent	quiet
cordial	intellectual	skeptical
cooperative	joking	sincere
defensive	inquisitive	shy
enthusiastic		

In general, there was a strong positive influence if the interviewer felt that the applicant was composed, cordial, cooperative, enthusiastic, and sincere. And most employers gave strong positive ratings to an interview that seemed relaxed, professional and balanced.[5]

Throughout this survey, the employers rated the critical factors under survey with reactions from strong positive to mild positive to mild negative to strong negative. While scholastic achievements were rated, personal characteristics and other related factors were also evaluated.

KEY FACTOR TO REMEMBER

Based on the two surveys, you, as a potential employee, should reflect upon and consider the employers' emphasis on the positive intangibles as brought to light in the Oahu survey, as well as the critical factors which were evaluated in the Mainland survey.

HUMAN RELATIONS – GETTING ALONG WITH SUPERVISORS, FELLOW EMPLOYEES AND THE PUBLIC

As indicated by the responses from the Oahu survey, the affective factors, those having to do with positive human relations, were emphasized by employers. Simply, this means that positive attitudes and behavior in human relations are desired in employees. While the Oahu survey was focused upon two-year college graduates, and the Mainland survey shed light on some human relations factors relating to four-year college graduates, there is no reason to believe that employers would not react in the same manner to non-college graduates. Positive human relations cut across all occupational clusters and this is one employability trait desired by employers.

Don't you want to work with people you can get along with? Well, so do employers. In fact, personnel situations and problems, including the major personnel problem of morale, are of deep concern to employers. Productivity, working relationships and other business concerns can be affected by the morale of a company's employees. Many job seekers may feel that they can get along with others in a work setting, but when values and personalities clash – especially on issues relating to duties, responsibilities, personal, controversial subjects and other matters, the non-positive reactions surface. The tolerance and adjustment factors wear thin in some cases. In normal employment interviews, adjustment, tolerance, and maturity are some of the intangibles which employers look out for. This does not mean that employers want workers who never disagree or who will never come into conflict with others. Disagreements and conflicts are natural human reactions, but when potential employees are sensed to be immature, irresponsible, unethical, inconsiderate, dishonest, and insufficient in ability to adjust to the mores of the work environment and people, employers react unfavorably. Most employers prefer not to hire anyone who possesses undesirable characteristics which hamper positive human relationships.

KEY FACTORS TO REMEMBER

The intangibles and personal traits revealed in the Oahu survey and partially in the Mainland survey indicate that such attributes are important factors in gaining employment. In view of this, ask yourself the following questions:

What do employers expect of me?
What are they looking for in me?
How does the employer view me?
Am I a reliable and responsible person?
How are my work habits?
What are my real attitudes?
Am I easy to communicate with?
Am I the silent type?
Am I pleasant?
Is my personality on the positive side?
Can I get along with
  my fellow workers?
  my supervisors?
  the general public?
Can I work under someone younger than I am?
Can I work under someone much older than I am?
Am I comfortable only with my own
  age group?
  sex group?
  racial group?
Will I adjust to a new environment?
Am I a willing listener and learner?

Management of employees with respect to human relations, morale, attitudes and work potential is an important area of concern for companies and institutions – and this involves intangibles, the positive character traits which employers prefer and seek out.

As a potential employee, reflect on the advantages of possessing positive traits, and if lacking, strive to work on positive self-development of characteristics employers desire.

INDUSTRIES AND BUSINESSES WITHIN THE JOB SEARCH AREAS

Part of the labor market information which you need is a thorough knowledge of the leading industries, the expanding industries, the emerging industries, the industries which are stabilized, and the industries which are phasing out. In addition, investigate the industries and businesses limited to specific localities.

Many industries and businesses exist only in a specific area. For example, the gambling and automobile industries are located in Nevada and Michigan, respectively, but not in Hawaii. Hawaii has no manufacturing industries in electronics, television or appliances, but has rather large industries in pineapple, sugar, tourism and support services vital to national defense, and coffee, which is grown and processed on the Island of Hawaii.

PINEAPPLE AND SUGAR

"Both the sugar and pineapple industries performed well in 1975."[6] However, in recent years acreage for sugar and pineapple production has declined;[7] and certain operational activities have been closed. There have also been recent lay offs in sugar. Prior to 1975, sugar production had experienced a slight 1.7 percent annual decline during the previous ten years,[8] and the pineapple canning tax base indicator had experienced a decline of activity by 2 percent annually during the previous nine years.[9]

"Although the value of output of the sugar and pineapple industries is declining in importance to the visitor and defense industries, these two basic agricultural industries accounted for nearly 15,000 jobs in 1975."[10] However, the outlook is that "agriculture employment will continue its gradual downward movement."[11] While these two industries in Hawaii have been stabilized in the past, the future outlook is less than positive.

TOURISM

Tourism in Hawaii thrives, but there are peaking and declining periods. Tourism is also Hawaii's major industry.[12] "It consists of a host of interrelated economic activities including hotels, transportation firms, travel agencies, tour operations, restaurants, portions of retail trade and entertainment groups."[13] Not to be excluded are the beach concessions and beach boys, night clubs, cocktail lounges, pedicabs, gift shops, scenic attractions and other businesses in the Waikiki area. Tourist attractions also exist in other locations on Oahu as well as on the Neighbor Islands.

DEFENSE

Defense is also considered to be a major industry which includes military bases, harbor and airports, communications network and roads.[14] "The annual growth of the defense expenditures is slowing down and it does not appear that defense will constitute a major source of future economic growth."[15]

GOVERNMENT

While government may not be an industry in the usual sense, a major source of employment in Hawaii is government —the Federal, State and County. The permanent jobs available within these three governmental jurisdictions are known as Civil Service or Merit System jobs. In Hawaii, government employment will increase slightly primarily from summer governmental contracts.[16] As the reader will remember, the sections on Civil Service as job sources in Chapter 1 gave data on numbers of job applicants hired by the three levels of government.

CONSTRUCTION

Construction activity was up only slightly in 1975,[17] and "employment in construction is expected to start a sluggish recovery up to September 1977."[18] During 1975, construction costs for high-rise buildings and single-family residences rose by 9.2 percent and 6.7 percent respectively, indicating an actual real gain of about 2 percent, but construction activity was down drastically in the residential market due to economic and other factors.[19]

"In the area of housing, the number of new private housing units authorized by building permits dropped sharply to 8,566 units versus 18,590 in 1974, a decrease of 54 percent."[20]

MANUFACTURING

Most of Hawaii's manufacturing is concentrated in Honolulu with 612 establishments listed in the City and County of Honolulu.[21] Food processing, including production of sugar, pineapple and fruit juices, is the largest manufacturing classification.[22] Heavy manufacturing includes two oil refineries, two cement plants, a steel mill for reinforcing rods, and 19 concrete product plants.[23] An outlook is that "manufacturing employment will continue its gradual downward movement."[24]

RESEARCH AND DEVELOPMENT

Research and development activity is expanding rapidly in Honolulu, particularly in the fields of oceanography, geophysics and bio-medicine.[25] Research and development activities involve participation of government agencies, private institutions, and the University of Hawaii. In private industry, prawn has emerged as a product of acquaculture and is being commercialized.

AIR AND SEA TRANSPORTATION

Air and sea transportation provide the business of the major airport and harbors. Honolulu International Airport was one of the busiest airports in the nation in 1974, handling 305,724 aircraft movements, with eight major domestic airlines providing several hundred flights per week between Honolulu and the Mainland.[26] Two scheduled airlines, air taxi and charter companies provide inter-island flights.[27] Honolulu is the primary mid-Pacific port for both air and sea lanes.

Many cargo steamship companies operate through Honolulu, and passenger service is provided by one domestic and several foreign lines.[28] In addition, a new Boeing Jetfoil Sea Ferry service has been operating since mid-1975 in inter-island waters, ferrying passengers and cargo.[29]

TRANSPORTATION, COMMUNICATION, UTILITIES, FINANCE, INSURANCE AND REAL ESTATE

"Transportation, communication and utilities may experience a slight rise," and "finance, insurance and real estate will experience some mixed trends." [30]

Small employment gains are anticipated in transportation, communication and utilities to September, 1977.[31]

RETAIL AND WHOLESALE

"Both retail and wholesale trades are expected to add to their payrolls substantially by fiscal year 1977."[32] This projection of employment increases is anticipated from expansion of existing shopping centers on Oahu and the addition of a few small centers on the Neighbor Islands.[33]

OVERVIEW

While the given information is pertinent to Hawaii, similar types of industries and businesses exist in practically every large city and state. Nearly every community has shopping centers, department stores, specialty and gift shops, super markets, radio and television stations, insurance companies, newspapers, service stations, banks, drug stores, hospitals, hotels, restaurants, hardware stores, union and non-union establishments, airports, universities, colleges and schools, and other businesses. In essence, these are the basic businesses and services required in any city, town and large community.

Private industries and businesses exist and proliferate, in response to the economy, supply and demand, and other complicating factors. They are significant to the job seeker in that varied types of jobs exist in these industries and businesses. For instance, nearly every industry or business operates with administrative, management, clerical, sales and other support personnel. Efficient secretaries and typists are indispensable to the business world. Technical firms and organizations require a staff of skilled and semi-skilled workers in fields such as plumbing, carpentry, drafting, general contracting, operating equipment and machinery, maintenance, and others.

As a job seeker, you should investigate and be familiar with all industries and businesses for possible positions.

JOB TRENDS

Employment trends vary and fluctuate in Hawaii as in any other locale. They are important to the job seeker because they serve as indicators of job availability. Resources of the civil service agencies and the state agencies such as the Hawaii State Employment Service and public libraries provide information sources on job trends. Information on current and projected job trends can be acquired readily here in Hawaii, as in any other State.

An example of a job trend in Hawaii is that there is an over supply of teachers and Hawaii's employment trends indicate a tight labor market for elementary and secondary school teachers, and a low turnover rate.[34] Currently, nearly all recent college graduates with educational majors in Hawaii are confronted with a depressed job market.[35] Anticipated additional positions plus the customary turnover rates projected approximately 200 jobs for teachers for the 1975-76 fiscal year, but with an oversupply of 3,500 applicants, the job outlook appears to be bleak for educational majors in Hawaii.[36]

Counselors in general will find great difficulty in seeking suitable employment in their field.

National trends similarly indicate that kindergarten, elementary and secondary school teacher job applicants, including college and university teaching candidates, face keen competition through the mid 1980s.[37] The supply of teacher job seekers far exceeds the job vacancies. Eventually many of these teachers will have to seek non-academic employment.[38]

National job trends also indicate that "employment of school counselors is likely to continue to grow more slowly than the average for all occupations through the mid 1980s as decline in school enrollment continues during the remainder of this decade."[39]

The job trend for clerical help in Hawaii in general is good; however, good skills and other positive assets are concommitant with this need. Skilled clerical job seekers have a better chance of obtaining jobs, but good pay rates are minimal in the entree positions. On the other hand, the actual job vacancies in this field are much fewer than the availability of job seekers. As projected, up through the latter part of 1977, clerical workers in Hawaii will continue to be one of the largest occupational categories.[40]

National job trends indicate also that the "employment of clerical workers is expected to increase faster than the average for all occupations through the mid 1980s."[41] In other words, prospects in clerical occupations are good.

In Hawaii, with respect to the growth of business organizations, in size and complexity, there will be a corresponding growth in recordkeeping which will generate opportunities for secretaries, stenographers, typists, cashiers, stock clerks and other clerical workers.[42]

With the demand for managers, officials and proprietors, this occupational category will be the fastest growing through September 1977.[43] This need will be linked mainly to expansions within the services industry where one out of three managers, officials and proprietors are employed.[44]

Due to the gradual shift of emphasis from goods-producing to service-producing industries, there will be a parallel shift in employment toward white collar occupations such as professional, technical, managerial, clerical and sales work.[45]

Less than ideal conditions have forced an increasing number of architects, drafters, carpenters, masons and others associated with the building trades into the ranks of the unemployed.[46]

A graphic example of the surplus of job applicants in Hawaii is the following list which "reflects the most intensively competitive areas where job seekers far outpaced the availability of job opportunities:"[47]

Professional, Technical and Managerial:
- Service Industry Management

Clerical:
- Secretarial Work
- Cashiering
- Stock Checking and Related Work

Sales:
- Sales Clerking

Service:
- Food Serving
- Bartending
- Cooking, large Hotels and Restaurants
- Cleaning and Related Services

Structural:
- Carpentry and Related Work
- Heavy Truck Driving

In a similar report of 1975, a surplus of job seekers was also reflected as follows:[48]

- Public Relations
- Elementary and Secondary Teachers
- Hostess/Host and Waitress/Waiter
- Kitchen Helper and Pantry Worker
- Aircraft
- Construction Worker
- Light Truck Driving

While other specific occupations have not been mentioned, there can still be the safe assumption that many other occupations have more applicants competing for these positions than there are positions available. One element contributing to worker surpluses is the steady influx of job seekers into this state.

How can the job seeker contend with this situation? One way is to seek out informational sources on job trends and to direct more attention to less competetive occupations. Resources of Federal, State and County agencies are easily accessible. Information on current and projected trends and hard-to-fill jobs can be readily acquired here in Hawaii.

Competition and a tight labor market require you, as the job seeker, to become familiar not only with the cluster occupations (related or similar type work) of your interest but with other occupational cluster groups as well.

PAY RATES

The prevailing wage rates offered within the community and in the job seeker's occupational interests should be an important acquisition of knowledge.

The minimum hourly wage by State Law is currently $2.40. The Federal minimum hourly wage is $2.30, except for employees earning tips as part of their work.

In Hawaii, pay rates vary in private industry and within three governmental civil service systems. While the state and county civil service salary schedules are uniform, the Federal civil service salary schedule differs. In addition, the Federal salary scale does grant a cost-of-living allowance to most of Hawaii's Federal employees.

The state civil service governs state employees on all of the inhabitable islands, except Niihau. There are four separate county civil service juridictions: Oahu, Hawaii, Maui and Kauai. These county civil service jurisdictions govern only those civil service positions within each of the individual counties. While the county civil service systems are autonomous, the salary schedules and fringe benefits, including retirement and other benefits offered to their civil service employees, are standardized throughout the islands. In fact, the salary schedules and job benefits are uniform with that of the state's civil service system. Collective bargaining has created a uniformity of pay and fringe benefits within the state and county civil service systems. Pay increases and benefits are dependent upon collective bargaining and state legislative action.

Prevailing pay rates for specified positions within each of the three levels of governmental civil service structures are a matter of public record and can be acquired from these agencies.

An extensive annual survey of pay rates is conducted in Hawaii by the Hawaii Employers Council relative to private industry and some governmental agencies. Entitled *Pay Rates in Hawaii,* this study is a good source of pay rate information for the various private industries and selected occupations in Hawaii.[49] In the last survey, 630 private firms and 15 government agencies were surveyed,[50] as were 8 major industry groupings,[51] and 109 job classifications.[52] Included in the government agency grouping was the non-appropriated fund military exchange system.[53] The 8 major industrial groupings surveyed were sugar, pineapple, trade, utilities and transportation, finance, manufacturing, service and miscellaneous.[54] The selected jobs surveyed for pay rates were within the clerical, trade, technical and professional occupations,[55] and the number of jobs reported for this survey totaled 51,585.[56]

Specific job descriptions were given in this survey, including a listing of the industries employing such occupations, as well as data on the full range of the pay rates, the mid 50% range, the median and the mean of the pay rates surveyed.

As an example, a study of clerk-stenographers in private industry revealed that the average wage earned on Oahu was $689 per month; that the full salary range was from $431 to $1,180 per month;[57] and that the overall average minimum and average maximum for private industry in Hawaii were $578 and $817 respectively.[58]

Other current and meaningful pay rate data can be found in this publication.

WORK FORCE IN HAWAII

During 1975, the annual average total civilian labor force* for the State of Hawaii was pegged at 356,440 and, for the Honolulu Standard Metropolitan Statistical Area (SMSA), at 286,460.[59] The annual average civilian labor force for the counties of Hawaii, Maui and Kauai were at 32,030, 23,370 and 14,580 respectively.[60]

The annual average civilian employment in Hawaii during this same period was calculated at 330,760, and for the Honolulu SMSA, at 266,900.[61] During this same period, the annual average civilian employment in the Hawaii County was 29,280, Maui County at 21,190 and Kauai County at 13,390.[62] Honolulu is situated on Oahu, and Oahu constitutes over four- fifths of all employed civilian persons in the State.[63]

An average annual breakdown by industry for 1975 of the total number of wage and salary jobs in the State of Hawaii and for the Honolulu SMSA are as follows: (figures rounded to hundreds)[65]

	State of Hawaii	Honolulu SMSA
Construction	28,180	24,160
Manufacturing	23,920	17,360
Transportation, Communications and Utilities	25,360	21,380
Trades	84,410	71,970
Finance, Insurance and Real Estate	23,290	21,090
Hotels	19,030	12,280

*The civilian labor force is defined as the total labor force exluding those individuals in the armed forces, i.e., all civilians, 16 years and over, classified as employed or unemployed. The employed is a count of the total number of individuals who are working in Hawaii, regardless of how many jobs a single individual may have, and is defined as those who: work as paid employees, or work in their own business, profession, or farm, or work at least 15 hours as unpaid family workers in a family operated enterprise; are not working but have jobs or businesses from which they are temporarily absent; work and are citizens of a foreign country, temporarily in the United States, and are not living on the premises of an Embassy.[64]

	State of Hawaii	Honolulu SMSA
Other Services	52,950	47,280
Federal Government (includes Postal workers)	30,530	29,680
State Government	38,700	31,700
Local or County Government	12,750	9,430
Agriculture	11,043	2,760

Other work force figures* show that the full-time Federal employees in Hawaii as of March 31, 1976, were comprised of 23,826 workers.[66] Previous years reflected slightly higher figures,[67] but defense activities have decreased.

Recent figures for the Honolulu County Civil Service as of June 1976, show that there are 12,848 people employed by this county, however, this figure includes Federally funded Concentrated Employment Training Act (CETA) employees, State funded State Comprehensive Employment and Training Program (SCET) employees, and the Mayor's Summer Youth Program Enrolees.[68] Of this number, only 6,996 are permanent Civil Service employees.[69]

The Hawaii State civil service work force numbered 16,048 during the 1975-1976 fiscal year.[70]

A publication, *Hawaii's Scientific Resources,* records employment of 31,624 persons† by 367 companies or agencies engaged in scientific activities in Hawaii.[71] As an example, the 26 governmental and private testing laboratories mentioned in this publication employ 972 persons, including 272 professionals and 243 technicians; and 8,318 persons are recorded as being employed by the 115 Federal, State and County agencies engaged in various scientific activities.[72]

*Includes General Schedule Wage Systems and the Postal Service.

†Due to certain refinements in, or changes in interpretation of, category definitions, which have led to a few sharp increases or decreases in certain employment listings compared with previous data, this and other figures presented call for cautious interpretation.[76]

A report which appraises the labor market conditions of women workers can be found in *Women Workers in Hawaii.* [73] While data in this report reflects the 1970 period, the employment status, labor force, and other appraisals are included in this report–including a projection of a continued increase in labor force participation by women. [74] During the 1970 period, women workers constituted 122,924, or 41.3 percent of the total civilian work force. [75]

Annual averages of the civilian labor force and employment for Hawaii from 1970 to 1976 can be found in the *Labor Market Indicators,* a publication of the Department of Labor and Industrial Relations. [77]

While these are only statistics which will fluctuate throughout the years, the job seeker can visualize the work force within these catagories. They can also sense the numbers of job applicants attempting to enter these fields, and of job seekers who are more available than the number of job openings in the listed industrial categories.

UNEMPLOYMENT IN HAWAII

The current unemployment rate of the community or locale has an effectively adverse influence in job seeking and the availability of jobs and should bc rcalized.

During the calendar year 1975, there was an annual average unemployment rate in Hawaii of 7.2 percent, which meant that 25,680 job seekers were unemployed.[78] And during this same year, there was an annual average of 19,560 job seekers unemployed on Oahu, or in the Honolulu SMSA.[79] In the three counties of Hawaii, Maui and Kauai, there were 6,120 job seekers unemployed.[80] The unemployment rate for the State of Hawaii for August 1976, was 9.0 percent, while the National Annual average unemployment rate for this same month was 7.6 percent.[81] In 1975, the annual average unemployment national rate was 8.5 percent.[82]

During 1974, Hawaii suffered an annual average unemployment rate of 7.6 percent.[83] In terms of jobless workers, 1974 showed an all time high (compared with previous years) with 27,400 persons out of work.[84]

Compared to the nation, Hawaii has a very high unemployment rate. According to national unemployment classification, there are six categories ranging from Group A, overall labor shortage of less than 1.5 percent unemployed, to Group F, substantial unemployment - 12 percent or higher.[85] Hawaii since April 1974, has been classed in Group D, a substantial unemployment labor area.[86]

JOB TURNOVER FACTORS

Job turnover, or how vacancies occur when previously filled, is caused by a multiplicity of factors, and awareness of these turnovers can potentially serve to benefit you as a job seeker.

The what, how and why of job turnover factors, or situations which create or help to create job turnover are as follows: (not necessarily in order of highest rate)

Retirement
Resignation or quits
Fires or discharges
Termination of contracts
Death
Prolonged sickness and/or disabilities
Promotions
Demotions
Transfers
Maternity leaves
Educational leaves
Military leaves
Marriages
Disappearances
Migrations

Job openings do occur when the following situations arise in the Hawaii labor market:

- Evolving new industries and businesses
- Expansion of industries and businesses
- Seasonal fluctuations in demands for services and products, such as in Tourism, hotels and restaurants, agriculture, Christmas holidays, and other occasions
- New or renewed Federal, State and/or County contracts
- Expansion of educational systems
- Expansion of governmental services
- Convening of the Hawaii State Legislature
- Foreign investments and businesses

OVERVIEW OF UNIONS

Brief information about unions may be of value to the job seeker. Unions have made inroads into the Federal Civil Service. Postal workers have been unionized as well. The Hawaii state and county civil service employees are unionized. Public educational sectors, comprised of the instructional, non-instructional and other support staff of the Department of Education and the University of Hawaii System have their own unions. A Hawaii Collective Bargaining Law is in effect for all employees of the Hawaii state and county governments.

The sugar and pineapple industries have been unionized. Most of the "Class A" hotels near and off the beach fronts on Oahu have been unionized,[87] as well as some of the larger hotels on the other islands. Other lesser hotels and some restaurants on Oahu have also been unionized.

The larger contracting firms also utilize members of various trade unions in construction work. Some workers in clerical, printing, food business, clothing, textile fields, musicians, workers in manufacturing, utility, sea, land and air transportation industries have also been unionized. While these sectors in private industry have been unionized, many have not.

As a potential source of inquiry or potential employment, unions should not be overlooked. You must remember that union members have priority in jobs within their respective unions, trades or occupations.

GENERAL OCCUPATIONAL INFORMATION

Occupational or vocational information generally concerns itself with the concepts, practices, literature, materials, references, and resources which exist to assist in the career planning, vocational choice and job search processes. It is about all aspects of the world of work: the who, what, where, why and how. Such information helps you, the job seeker, to orient and prepare yourself to enter the world of work and to progress in it. It helps you to gain the knowledge to motivate yourself positively in job seeking and to help you make vocational choices. Such information should help you to better understand occupations, occupational choices and interests, educational and training resources, job sources, the work environment, job search approaches, job seeking difficulties, employment rights and benefits, employment laws, including survival in the world of work. Chart 1, page 55, can provide you with a visual explanation of the terms occupational or vocational information as these relate to you.

The broad range of resource materials on occupational information can be found in public libraries, school and college libraries, college placement offices, and career development and counseling centers, and in bibliographies of books such as this. Publications of governmental agencies such as the State Department of Labor and Industrial Relations and its offices, the State Department of Planning and Economic Development, the U. S. Civil Service Commission, and the U. S. Labor Department are available.

When in doubt as to sources of specific information desired, do not hesitate to ask questions and seek out people sources for assistance.

CHART 1

RANGE OF OCCUPATIONAL INFORMATION AND THE VARIETY OF JOB SEEKERS

* Theories and research on work and vocational development
* Concepts of man and work
* Career planning
* Vocational choices and interests
* Educational and training resources
* Trends in business and industry
* Job trends
* Occupational clusters
* Job sources
* Job requirements
* Availability of jobs
* Employers
* Communication avenues of and within the world of work
* Work environment and conditions
* Unions
* Equal employment opportunity laws
* Preparation for job seeking
* Job seeking approaches
* Application forms and letters
* Resumes and other documents
* Human relations
* Self-assessment/self-inventory
* Employee fringe benefits
* Compensation
* Employee responsibilities
* Resources for assistance
* Competition for jobs
* Selectivity by employers
* Job interviews
* Barriers to employment
* Survival in the world of work

JOB SEEKERS

University students and graduates

Two-year College students and graduates

Business and Technical school students and graduates

Job ready
Qualified
Over qualified
Under qualified
School dropouts
Veterans
Minorities
Disadvantaged
Elderly
Professional
Blue collar
White collar
High school students
Housewives
Youths
Disabled
Different lifestyles
Prolonged absence from work force
Newcomers
Parolees

CHAPTER 3

OCCUPATIONS IN HAWAII WHICH NEED LICENSES, CERTIFICATES, REGISTRATION OR PERMITS

The job seeker should have a knowledge of occupations in Hawaii which require licensing, registration, certificates or permits for legal employment or business operations.*

The Hawaii State Department of Labor, in cooperation with other state agencies, has published a report, *Licensed Occupations in Hawaii,* which provides information on occupational requirements or standards for 41 occupations in Hawaii which require licenses or certificates.[1] These 41 and additional occupations and occupational requirements can also be found in a publication titled *Starting a Business in Hawaii,* published by the Department of Planning and Economic Development, State of Hawaii.[2]

In addition, certain occupations or positions in the state and county civil service do need special requirements before the job applicant can apply for these positions, such as possessing a Master of Social Work Degree (MSW) in order to qualify for a supervisor's position in social work. One must also, for example, have special qualifications and pass an examination in order to qualify for a position as a chemist in the State De-

---

* Most of the information on occupations, state licensing agencies, and county permit granting agencies was obtained from two publications, *Licensed Occupations in Hawaii* and *Starting a Business in Hawaii.* Other information on occupational licensing was extracted from the various state laws and rules and regulations which govern these occupations, and from consultation with considerate personnel of the state agencies, a Honolulu county agency, and the U.S. Coast Guard.

partment of Health. Possession of a Red Cross Senior Lifesaving Certificate and a Standard First Aid and Safety Certificate is necessary in order for an applicant to be considered for employment as a lifeguard with county agencies, institutions, and with private industry. New hours have been added to first aid training, and when accumulated, Red Cross Multimedia Certificates are issued. There are other positions in civil service which need some kind of certification in order for a job applicant to qualify for higher level positions.

The four separate county governments also approve and issue various types of business permits and licenses. Federal agencies also certify certain types of occupations.

STATE LICENSING AGENCIES AND OCCUPATIONS

The Hawaii State Department of Regulatory Agencies regulates most of the licensing and certifications. Different State boards and commissions, housed within this agency, actually oversee licensing and certification according to Hawaii State Laws, as do other state agencies. As part of their authority, the State agencies, boards and commissions set the occupational standards and requirements, examination requirements, temporary permit or certificate requirements, and fee requirements, as well as provide occupational definitions.[3]

A compiled list of numerous occupations which need official approval and their licensing or permit granting state agencies is as follows:

PROFESSIONAL AND VOCATIONAL LICENSING DIVISION, HAWAII STATE DEPARTMENT OF REGULATORY AGENCIES

Abstract Maker
Acupuncture
Architect
Barber
Boiler Mechanic

State licensing agencies continued. . .

- Boxing occupations:
  - Boxer
  - Second
  - Manager
  - Trainer
  - Referee
  - Judge
  - Timer
  - Announcer
  - Physician
  - Matchmaker
  - Promoter - Professional
  - Promoter - Amateur
- Cemetery Salesperson
- Cemetery Pre-need Funeral Salesperson
- Certified Public Accountant
- Chiropractor
- Collector (collection agency)
- Contractor
- Cosmetologist:
  - Instructor
  - Cosmetician
  - Electrologist
  - Manicurist
  - Cosmetic Technician
- Dental Hygienist
- Dentist
- Detective, Private
- Detective, Guard
- Drivers: (Public Utility Certificate)
  - Limousines
  - Taxi Cabs
  - Tour Buses
  - Trucks
  - School Buses (and others)

State licensing agencies continued...

Electrician
Elevator Mechanic
Engineer
Hearing Aid Dealer and Fitter
Insurance Salesperson
Landscape Architect
Land Surveyor
Masseur/Masseuse
Mortgage Broker
Motion Picture Operator
Motor Vehicle Salesperson
Motor Vehicle Mechanic
Motor Vehicle Mechanic's Helper
Naturopath
Nurse (R.N.)
Nurse, Practical
Nursing Home Administrator
Optician
Optometrist
Osteopath
Pest Control Operator
Pharmacist
Physician (Doctor of Medicine)
Physician (Naturopath)
Plumber
Psychologist
Public Accountant
Real Estate Broker
Real Estate Salesperson
Security Salesperson
Stock Broker
Speech Pathologist and Audiologist
Travel Agency Sales Representative
Veterinarian

State licensing agencies continued. . .

HAWAII STATE DEPARTMENT OF HEALTH

Embalmer
Sanitarian
Tattoo Artist
Physical Therapist
Nurse-Midwife
Clinical Laboratory Director
Clinical Laboratory Supervisor
Clinical Laboratory Technologist, or Specialist
Cytotechnologist
Clinical Laboratory Technician
Food Service Establishment Workers: *
- Waitress/Waiter
- Cook
- Kitchen Helper
- Bartender
- Managerial personnel
- Other food and liquor handling workers

HAWAII STATE ATTORNEY GENERAL'S OFFICE

Notary Public

HAWAII STATE DEPARTMENT OF SOCIAL SERVICES AND HOUSING

Babysitting
Boarding Homes
(for Social Services clientele)

---

* The State Health Department issues "Health Clearance Certificates" to applicants upon presentation of a Doctor's Health Certificate and proof of X- ray which certifies to satisfactory health conditions; for workers who handle liquor, presentation of "Health Clearance Certificates" are made to the County Liquor Commission for the issuance of Yellow Card Registration work permits. Blue Card Registrations are issued to managerial personnel.

State licensing agencies continued. . .

HAWAII STATE DEPARTMENT OF EDUCATION

Teacher, Elementary
Teacher, Secondary
Substitute Teacher
Counselor
School Librarian
Speech and Hearing Specialist
Psychological Examiner
Media Specialist
Special Education Teacher

CHILD LABOR SECTION, ENFORCEMENT DIVISION, HAWAII STATE DEPARTMENT OF LABOR AND INDUSTRIAL RELATIONS

Teenagers, 14-17 (Work Permits)

HAWAII STATE SUPREME COURT

Attorney [4]

DIVISION OF OCCUPATIONAL SAFETY AND HEALTH, HAWAII STATE DEPARTMENT OF LABOR AND INDUSTRIAL RELATIONS

Blaster

HAWAII STATE DEPARTMENT OF TAXATION

State Gross Income License

FEDERAL CERTIFYING AGENCIES AND OCCUPATIONS

U.S. COAST GUARD

Coast Guard Certificates are needed for the following people who sail on U.S. Flag Vessels:

Seaman
Harbor Pilot
Motor Boat Operator
Charter Boat Operator
Pleasure Craft Operator
Blaster

IMMIGRATION AND NATURALIZATION SERVICE, U.S. DEPARTMENT OF JUSTICE;

Foreign students on F-I Visas desiring part-time or summer employment must apply to the Immigration and Naturalization Service in order to be given permission to seek work. Permission to obtain on-the-job training, or work related to study or educational requirements must also be granted by this Federal agency. While work related to academic requirements is usually valid, foreign students must be able to justify the need to seek part-time work. Depending on annual rulings of this Federal agency, summer employment may be permitted with fewer restrictions. In these work situations, the agency requires that the employment of foreign students should not displace Americans seeking the same jobs. However, generally, the application for permission to seek work should first be made to the college or university where the students are enrolled. East-West Center grantees and spouses with visas need the consent of the University of Hawaii.

Persons on official Refugee Status may seek work, provided approval is officially granted by the Immigration and Naturalization Service.

COUNTY BUSINESS/OCCUPATIONAL PERMITS

DIVISION OF LICENSES, HONOLULU COUNTY

Auctioneer
Boarding House
Pawnbroker
Peddler - Cake
Peddler - Merchandise or Medicine
Second-Hand Dealer
Baggage or Freight Vehicle for hire
Passenger Vehicle
Solicitor
Selling Game Bird Carcass or Parts
Itinerant Vendor
Taxicab
Dealer in Used Vehicle Parts and Accessories
Rebuilding Motor Vehicles for Resale
Wrecking, Salvaging and Dismantling
Auto Driving Instructor
U-Drive
Storage and Sale of Fireworks
Collection of Garbage and/or Rubbish
Dance School
Chauffeur (by Honolulu Police Department)
Operator (by Honolulu Police Department)

OTHER COUNTIES

The Hawaii, Maui and Kauai counties issue similar types of business licenses as those issued by the Honolulu County.

OVERVIEW

The lists of occupations and business permits given are not by any means exhaustive as there are Federal agencies which license airline pilots and crew members, radio and television broadcasters, and other occupational classes. More recently, the County required registration of Pedi-Cabs which are quite visible in the Waikiki area.

The requirements for the granting of permits and licenses range from the most minimal to very rigid standards and requirements. The factors taken into consideration for occupational licensing are based on education, training, experience, age, personal character, residency, bonding, fee requirements and other considerations, depending upon the specific occupation involved.

Since many occupations require licenses and certificates to meet State, County and Federal requirements, persons should check with the proper agency for full occupational information. Licensing and business requirements and regulations should be obtained from the proper agency sources and understood.

The Federal "Dictionary of Occupational Titles" (DOT), Volume I, is useful in that it contains general definitions of the listed occupations. Volume I has the titles and definitions of 21,741 separate occupations arranged alphabetically according to job title.[5] While titles may vary, definitions for these job titles are provided. The DOT is available in public employment agencies, college and university placement offices, and should be available in college, university and public libraries.

CHAPTER 4

JOB SEEKING APPROACHES

There is no one method in job seeking. The effectiveness of each method utilized depends upon the applicant's initiative, resources, organization, personal attitudes, personal motivation, persistence and knowledge of job sources.

JOB SEEKING METHOD SURVEY BY THE U.S. DEPARTMENT OF LABOR

The Manpower Administration, U.S. Department of Labor, financed a nationwide survey in 1973 conducted by the Bureau of Census to determine job search methods used by Americans and the effectiveness of the various methods used.[1] The survey covered:

> Nearly 16 million wage and salary workers 16 years old and over who were not in school and who had started their current jobs during 1972. About 5.5 million of these workers had not found it necessary to look for work because they returned to jobs held formerly, were offered jobs, had entered a family business, or other reasons. Of the 10.4 million who actively sought work, about half began their search either as new entrants or reentrants to the labor force. The remainder had lost or quit their jobs or wanted to change jobs.[2]

A preliminary analysis of the results of the survey showed that:[3]

1) The method most commonly used by all job seekers, by 2 out of 3, was direct application to employers without suggestions or referrals by anyone.
2) Direct application was also named by the largest proportion of workers as the method by which they found their present jobs. Next in rank were: Asking friends about jobs where they work, and answering local newspaper ads.
3) About half of all persons who applied directly to employers for work found their current jobs that way, about double the percentage for the methods with the next two highest rates.

After listing all the methods by which they used to find work, respondents were then asked to select from the list the method by which they obtained their present job and the three top-ranking methods used were:[4]

1) Direct application to employers.
2) Asking friends about jobs.
3) Answering advertisements in newspapers.

"About the same proportion of workers found jobs through the State employment service as through private employment agencies."[5]

As defined, "the effectiveness of each job search method may be expressed as the proportion of persons using it who obtained their current jobs by that method."[6] "The method with the highest effectiveness rate by far, was application directly to an employer – 48 percent of all persons who used this method reported that they had obtained their job that way."[7]

The most effective method of direct application to employers was followed by six others which had effectiveness rates about half that of direct application: Private agencies, local newspaper ads, asking friends about jobs where they work, union hiring halls, school placement services and asking relatives about jobs where they work.[8]

The most effective job search method, next to applying directly to an employer, also varied sharply by occupation in that the hiring hall was the second most effective for craft workers, operatives, and non-farm laborers.[9] Local newspaper ads had the second highest rate for managers and administrators, transport equipment operatives, sales workers, and service workers; while school placement offices were the second most effective for professional and technical workers and the private employment agency was the second most effective means used for clerical workers.[10]

There is some implication in this Federal survey that many persons were sufficiently reliant and had a command of techniques sufficient to get jobs. While the standard job sources such as the public and private employment agencies, relatives and friends, newspaper want ads and agency and institutional resources were sought out, it can be surmised that self reliance reinforced with job search knowledge and the motivation to get jobs, were the individual strengths used most effectively by these job seekers in finding employment. And on the average, the workers surveyed used four methods to seek jobs.[11]

JOB SEARCH METHODS USED IN HAWAII

In Hawaii, the following methods are used singularly and in combination: (not necessarily in order of highest use)

Applying directly to employers
Asking family, relatives and friends
Following through on help wanted ads
Utilizing services of State employment agencies
Utilizing services of other governmental agencies
Applying for Federal, State and County positions
Seeking political influence
Utilizing services of private employment agencies
Advertising skills and services to employers in newspapers and other printed sources
Asking association or organization members

Checking with unions
Entering a family business
Checking with placement offices
Checking with teachers
Checking with counselors
Seeking out private institutions dealing with human services
Utilizing equal employment opportunity laws
And, utilizing other resources deemed most effective for the job seeker

KEY FACTORS TO REMEMBER

When seeking employment, the environment you enter may contain different values than those you have expected. In order to compete for jobs, you will encounter situations, or will be required to do things which you may dislike or may not be used to. You will discover that hiring practices are not standardized and that various methods must be utilized to get jobs. In your job search, you must know and tap all available sources for assistance in finding jobs.

To recapitulate, you will remember that the most effective means employed by job seekers in which they found their present jobs, according to the U.S. Department of Labor survey, were: Applying directly to employers, asking friends about jobs, answering advertisements in newspapers, seeking services of public and private employment agencies, checking with unions, seeking out school placement offices and asking relatives about jobs. You should utilize these methods and employ other means in the job search.

Ask yourself, simply and objectively, what methods should I utilize? What approaches are most viable in my situation? What will be the most effective means for me? Which of the following techniques are most applicable for me?

Positive, direct approaches to employers?
Asking family, relatives and friends?

Demonstrating skills, work potential, sense of creativity, and other personal assets?
Using personal and political influence?
Relying on job quotas based on minority status, sex, and other factors?
Responding to want ads?
Seeking out governmental and private agency sources?
Advertising to employers?
Checking with unions and with fellow members?
Relying on a combination of approaches?

The job seeker can utilize whatever initiative, resources and means deemed best in a given situation. Hiring practices vary. Given this situation, the job applicant should be flexible and experiment with a variety of methods and approaches. If the job is competitive, the applicant should expand job search methods utilized and capitalize upon personal assets and use of influence.

To re-emphasize, perhaps a point in reality can be expressed by commenting that the more competitive the job, the more effective the results to obtain a job through the use of influence. While "word of mouth" advertising through friends and relatives and other questionable means of favoritism in filling jobs are frowned-upon practices, especially with agencies and organizations which receive Federal grants, these practices do prevail.

As an added discussion of job seeking methods, perhaps the term ethics should be discussed as it concerns hiring practices and job seeking as these exist. Ethics in both situations is conditional or situational. Respective of the employer and job seeker, it is action taken in a given employment situation. Ethics in hiring practices depends on the employer's expectations, personal attitudes, business and personal obligations, job and personal requirements of the position and applicant, business/institutional needs, adherence to Equal Employment Opportunity Laws, hiring quotas based on race/sex and other factors.

Ethics in job seeking is identified in terms of approaches or methods utilized, avenues of access sought, sources employed, qualification/abilities/potentials demonstrated, energies expended, motivation used, attributes displayed, as well as personal attitudes, sense of personal ethics, conscience, personal sacrifices and other considerations.

In essence, there is no one practice in hiring ethics and no one practice in job seeking ethics.

CHAPTER 5

SELF-ASSESSMENT AND SELF-INVENTORY

Self-assessment is defined as evaluating one's attitudes, personality characteristics, beliefs, tolerance levels, sense of values, common sense, maturity, lifestyle, motivation, and other basic intrinsic values. In other words, all of the intangibles of the job seeker which employers can feel, sense or react to.

Self-inventory is defined as an analysis of one's employability, skills, qualifications, abilities, work potential and past work experiences; and an analysis of unrelated job aspects of personal earned achievements, accomplishments, past life experience and other attributes.

Self-assessment and self-inventory processes assist the job seeker in analyzing the total employability aspects which employers perceive in applicants. An objective analysis provides insight into employability characteristics possessed and allows the individual to make the necessary adjustments which will enhance employability.

However, to only be aware of one's self in terms of intrinsic values, qualifications, abilities, work potential and positive past life experiences is insufficient. Objectivity in self-assessment and self-inventory, as well as positive application of one's self, is important to enhance success in the job search. It guides the job seeker in establishing more effective and positive relationships with employers.

SELF-ASSESSMENT

Self-assessment involves an analysis of yourself as a potential employee in terms of your attitudes, beliefs, character, stability, maturity, sense of values, responsibilities, enthusiasm, motivation, and other personal traits or characteristics.

Color, size, age, sex and other hereditary factors cannot be altered, unless drastic measures are taken. Certain changes are beyond the normal control of job seekers. While hereditary aspects can seldom be changed, social, cultural and attitudinal conditioning can be modified.

Should the job seeker assume that a personal assessment is not necessary, for such reasons as: Employers have or will perceive the job seeker in a favorable light; an assessment for improvement or modification is not necessary; such a personal assessment is counter to personal belief; or a personal assessment will not really help, then the job seeker will most likely be minimizing chances for employment and will most likely not be properly prepared for all eventualities. In view of the job shortages, the competition and other factors, the job seeker should realistically assess the assumption and objectively reflect on whether or not a personal assessment will increase chances for jobs.

For the job seeker who feels that there is room for personal assessment to ascertain the possibilities of potential improvement or modification, two simple exercises performed objectively can help in the self-assessment process.

Assess yourself in the first exercise as though you sincerely believe that this is you as a person by checking off the proper categories in Chart 2,

CHART 2 A SELF-ASSESSMENT EXERCISE OF ONE'S QUALITIES

	Satisfactory	Fair-Can Be Better	Need Improvement	Don't Really Know
My attitude toward employers?				
My attitude toward work?				
My attitude toward work responsilbilities?				
My attitude toward strangers?				
My working relationship with fellow employees?				
My personal maturity?				
My tolerance of people? Open mindedness?				
My Personal Characteristics:				
Friendly?				
Courteous?				
Reliable?				
Honest? Truthful?				
Sincere?				
Enthusiastic?				
Considerate?				
Agressive?				

Assess yourself in the second exercise from the point of view of an employer assessing you. Check off the proper categories in Chart 3.

CHART 3

A SELF-ASSESSMENT EXERCISE OF HOW YOU BELIEVE AN EMPLOYER WILL RATE YOUR PERSONAL CHARACTERISTICS AND VALUES

	Satisfactory	Fair - Can Be Better	Need Improvement	Don't Really Know
Your attitude toward the employer?				
Your attitude toward the company?				
Your attitude toward being a responsible employee?				
Your attitude toward lesser wages offered?				
Your ability to work with other employees?				
Your capacity to do more than your share of the work?				
Your tolerance level? Are you open minded?				
Your maturity level?				
Your personality traits and characteristics:				
Your friendliness?				
Your courteousness?				
Your reliability?				
Your honesty?				
Your enthusiasm?				
Your consideration for others?				
Your emotional stability?				
Your agressiveness?				

THE VALUE OF SELF-ASSESSMENT

Basic attitudes and feelings evolve and are demonstrated, not so much in ordinary situations, but in critical or stress situations. Personal contact with employers or interviewers can potentially bring out such attitudes and behavior from the job seeker. Dogmatic, liberal, conservative, reactionary or neutral, whatever the attitudes, the job seeker should modify them when they are detrimental to employability. Potential jobs are at stake. The term modify strongly implies the need for adjustment of attitudes and approaches so as not to displease or turn off employers.

Lifestyles, beliefs, sense of responsibility, emotional and work stability, tolerance levels, sense of values, personality characteristics and other personal traits are to be carefully considered in the light of whether or not modifications are needed. Relate these to the reaction of others, especially employers, and ask yourself whether they are positive or non-positive attitudes and behavior, and whether they will enhance or be detrimental towards getting a job. Attitudes reflect values and when they surface, these values may run counter to the employer's personal sense of values.

Also ask yourself:

Are your real attitudes, when they surface, amenable with the expectations of employers?

What are your attitudes:

Toward work?

Toward employers?

Toward business and the profit system?

Toward duties and responsibilities as a potential employee?

Toward wages, employee benefits and work conditions offered, when less than expected?

Toward different ethnic or cultural groups?

Toward the business public?

Are your life style, behavioral patterns and other traits suitably presentable in contacts with employers? If not, should modification and improvements be made to assist in "turning on" employers?

In applicable situations, an equation can be visualized and be of some value in the self-assessment process.

DESIRE + COMPETITION = MODIFICATION? REWARD?

If improvements or modifications are needed and can be made, is it not a small price to pay for the potential reward of getting jobs? Viewed from another perspective, what price will be paid by you for unwillingness to adjust?

You are not being asked to make prolonged or permanent changes as an individual, nor are you being asked to relegate yourself to gross unpleasantries. You are only being advised to modify traits and characteristics deemed undesirable when employer contacts are made. In the final analysis, it is you who will have to decide for yourself. Perhaps Chart 4, page 77, "Motivation In The Job Search" can be of assistance to you. This Chart does not imply remedy, nor does it serve as a catalyst for action, but it does illustrate the processes and influences in the motivational process.

SELF-INVENTORY

When queried as to whether or not this writer was an expert in jobs, this writer facetiously answered yes, "I have been employed most of my life." So could a job seeker answer, orally and in writing, but seriously, to another kind of question, "Yes, I can handle telephone calls properly, for I have answered telephones most of my life." This is one application of a work potential in a given situation.

This section on self-inventory will discuss the inventories of: 1) work experience and abilities, and 2) positive past life experience.

To inventory all of one's employability assets is only one phase of preparation in seeking employment. To only list these employability attributes is insufficient. These personal assets must be fairly well organized and be applied in job searches.

CHART 4

MOTIVATION
IN THE JOB SEARCH

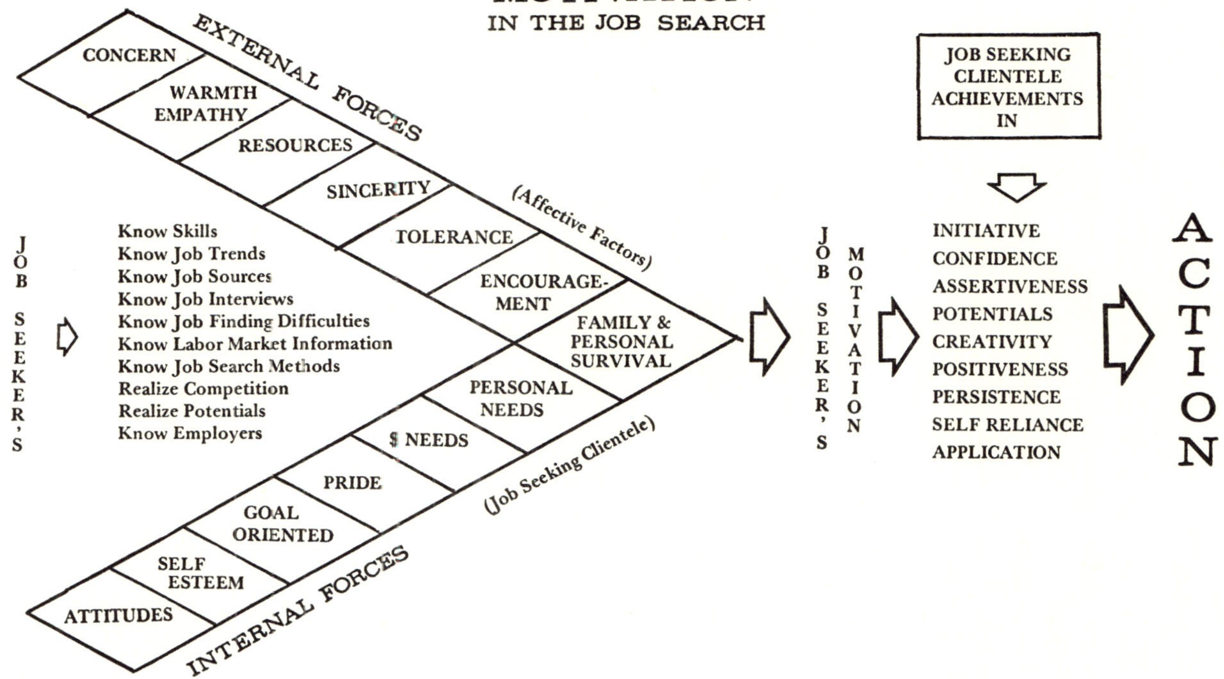

WORK EXPERIENCE – ANALYSIS AND INVENTORY

Work experience, qualifications, skills and abilities relating to employment have most likely been established and documented in one way or another, but possibly only in a relatively few occupational areas. As an example, a job seeker may have had skills and work experience driving large vans, heavy trucks or trailer trucks, but not in operating heavy construction vehicles and equipment. Or a job seeker may have had work experience in writing and editing technical subject matter, but not in researching or writing programs, or writing proposals for Federal grants. Or a job seeker may have had work experience as a telephone operator, but not as a receptionist.

Relating acquired skills, knowledge and work experiences to similar job vacancies is relatively easy. When jobs, however, become scarce or limited, and other positions are sought, a job seeker can translate personal acquisitions of skills, abilities and work experiences to other types of jobs. Assuming that construction equipment operator positions or machine maintenance positions are available, a truck driver could apply knowledge of combustion engines and driving or operating mechanisms learned to the operation of light or heavy construction vehicles and equipment, not only in construction but also in other industries. Other attributes such as the ability to work for prolonged hours, to assume responsibility for the care of expensive equipment, to work effectively and productively without supervision, conditioning in working alone, coordination and good reflexes, can be brought into play to enhance the job seeker's chances for jobs for which there has been no actual on-the-job work experience. No doubt, other attributes can also be brought into play.

A person who has written various types of technical reports has most probably performed research on facts, needs, priorities, has met deadlines and has probably read extensively on various subjects. The individual who has written technical works can translate writing skills, knowledge and personal qualities to other positions as a researcher, editor, consultant, program developer, news reporter, creative writer, public relations person, or other types of work involving literary skills.

Assets such as love of writing, reading and other literary interests can be emphasized when vying for other positions.

A receptionist, for example, is expected to be courteous, helpful, informative, patient, tactful, cheerful and possessed with other desirable personal qualities, including appearance. Such attributes and the faculty for memory can be applied by a person with only telephone work experience who is seeking receptionist or another type of job which requires pleasant public contact abilities.

Military experience also can be translated effectively into civilian employment. The *Military/Civilian Source Book*, a publication of the Department of Defense, can be used to relate Army, Navy, Air Force, Marine Corps and Coast Guard experience to civilian occupations. [1]

When analyzed, other translations and relationships of past work experience can be directed toward other types of jobs. A consideration can be free-lancing in a specialty.

In view of your work experience, skills and acquired knowledge, a simple listing of personal assets which can be applied in various work settings can be categorized and inventoried. Use Chart 5, page 80, to list your acquired assets:

PAST LIFE EXPERIENCES – ANALYSIS AND INVENTORY

You may have at one time or another, performed certain duties, or achieved certain distinctions or accomplishments in the social, economic, political, educational, domestic, recreational, or religious areas of life.

Past life experiences in unrelated employment situations can be utilized as assets when applied to the search for employment. These experiences may include all types of volunteer work such as serving as an officer or being a member of an association, helping to organize community events, assisting in human services programs, supporting Boy or Girl Scout movements, raising funds for worthy causes, rearing children, tutoring, actively engaging in hobbies, and a host of other meaningful

CHART 5

AN INVENTORY OF WORK EXPERIENCES, SKILLS, KNOWLEDGE, AND POTENTIALS, CIVILIAN AND MILITARY

QUALIFICATIONS: (training, education and others)

SKILLS:

ABILITIES:

KNOWLEDGE GAINED:

WORK POTENTIAL GAINED:

---

activities.

What were the gains of participation in the various activities which can be applied to a work setting?

Accepting responsibility
Being active and contributing to meaningful events
Organizing ability
Acquiring patience
Meeting people and establishing positive relationships
Working with all types of people
Dedicating hours and days, at times inconvenient, to accomplish tasks and goals

Participation and involvement in varied situations may not in themselves have produced these positive attributes, but perhaps they may have contributed toward the strengthening of these qualities.

A simple inventory of positive life experiences gained,

applicable in job seeking and to a potential work environment, can be categorized, inventoried and utilized. Using Chart 6, list your acquisitions:

CHART 6

AN INVENTORY OF POSITIVE PAST LIFE EXPERIENCES GAINED, UNRELATED TO EMPLOYMENT

MEMBERSHIP IN CLUBS, ASSOCIATIONS, AND OTHER ORGANIZATIONS: (in all areas of social, business, political, educational, recreational, military, domestic and religious)

INDIVIDUAL PEOPLE SOURCES: (personal, political, ethnic, business and other types of friendships gained)

LICENSES, CERTIFICATES, DEGREES EARNED: (in all areas)

SPECIFIC ACTIVITIES AND INVOLVEMENTS: (in all areas)

SPECIFIC ACHIEVEMENTS AND ACCOMPLISHMENTS: (in all areas)

OTHER MEANS OF ASSESSMENT AND INVENTORY

The *Dictionary of Occupational Titles (DOT), Volume II,* provides information on three work relationship areas which can assist job seekers in their self-assessment and self-inventory processes. This information is also useful for planning careers and making occupational choices. It realistically assesses job seekers' interests, aptitudes, capabilities, qualifications, potentials and other factors. . . . . . ."Based on the premise that every job requires a worker to function in relation to Data, People, and Things in varying degrees," these three relationships are identified and categorized in separate hierarchies, with each hierarchy, or order, arranged from relatively simple to complex categories of functions.[2]

For example, under the first section, *"People Hierarchy,"* the term *people* is defined as dealing with human beings and also dealing with animals on an individual basis as if they were human.[3] Under *"People Hierarchy"* are listed such functions as mentoring, negotiating, instructing, supervising, diverting, persuading, speaking-signaling, serving, and no significant relationship categories.[4] By reading this two-page section, a job seeker can gain some insight of self-potential by assessing these functions realistically in terms of aptitudes and potentials needed in working with people or with data or with things.

A second section deals with *"Worker Traits"* and provides more information. *"Worker Traits"* are those abilities, personal traits, and individual characteristics required of workers so that average successful job performance can be achieved.[5] These *"Worker Traits"* have been categorized under six basic components:[6]

1. Training time (includes general educational development and specific vocational preparation)
2. Aptitudes
3. Interests
4. Temperaments
5. Physical demands
6. Working Conditions

Each of these components is defined clearly for easy comprehension.

A third work relationship area is entitled *"Worker Trait Groups Within The Area Of Work."*[7] Twenty-two areas of work are explained and in each of these individual areas of work, additional occupations are listed.[8] For example, one of the twenty-two areas of work is clerical, and within this particular clerical work area, various groupings of related occupations are listed:[9]

1. Supervisory Work (clerical, sales, and related activities)
2. Scheduling, Dispatching, Expediting, and Related Work
3. Secretarial and Related Work
4. Corresponding and Related Work
5. Information Gathering, Dispensing, Verifying, and Related Work
6. Paying and Receiving (banks and other establishments)
7. Cashiering (drug stores, theaters, restaurants, and related establishments)

8 to 17. And other related occupations

Within a particular occupational group such as in supervisory work, *"Worker Traits"* are explained as follows:[10]

1. Work performed
2. Worker requirements
3. Clues for relating applicants and requirements
4. Training and methods of entry
5. Related occupations

This third work relationship category provides the job seeker with some guidelines for self-assessment and self-inventory, as well as meaningful information on related types of occupations.

You, as a job seeker, are not expected to interpret and translate technical matters in the *DOT* sections under discussion. A study of these three sections, however, can give you a perspective about yourself relative to employment.

Of course, assistance in the self-assessment and self-inventory processes from information provided in the *DOT* can be obtained from people resources such as from vocational counselors, placement personnel and others who are required to be knowledgeable about the *DOT* and matters relating to the self-assessment and self-inventory processes. Knowledge of the *DOT* is a basic tool to provide vocational guidance. These people resources can assist you not only in interpretation, but also in application of this information.

POSITIVE ORGANIZATION AND APPLICATION

In a tight labor market situation when desirable jobs are limited and highly competitive, other types of jobs should, and must be considered. Utilize your positive personal assets and expand your job search area by considering the following actions:

1. Extracting desired assets from the self-assessment analysis
2. Extracting salient acquisitions from the self-inventory assessments
3. Expanding your job search into related jobs or occupational clusters
4. Expanding your job search into unrelated occupational areas
5. Expanding your job search into other businesses and industries
6. Expanding your personal motivation and persistence

Chart 7, page 85, will provide you with an idea of possible entry into other occupations and industries.

When considering the positive results of the self-assessment and self-inventory processes, analyze your skills, experience, abilities and potential; assess your positive past life experience; and examine your present resources. Then explore the numerous related types of jobs and related and unrelated occupational clusters of jobs in the various businesses and industries. It is

CHART 7

GUIDANCE IN YOUR JOB SEARCH

Investigate Related As Well As Unrelated Or Desired And Undesired Job Objectives

Broaden Base Of Operation Toward Job Hunt And You Will Expand Your Objectives, Insight And Achievements

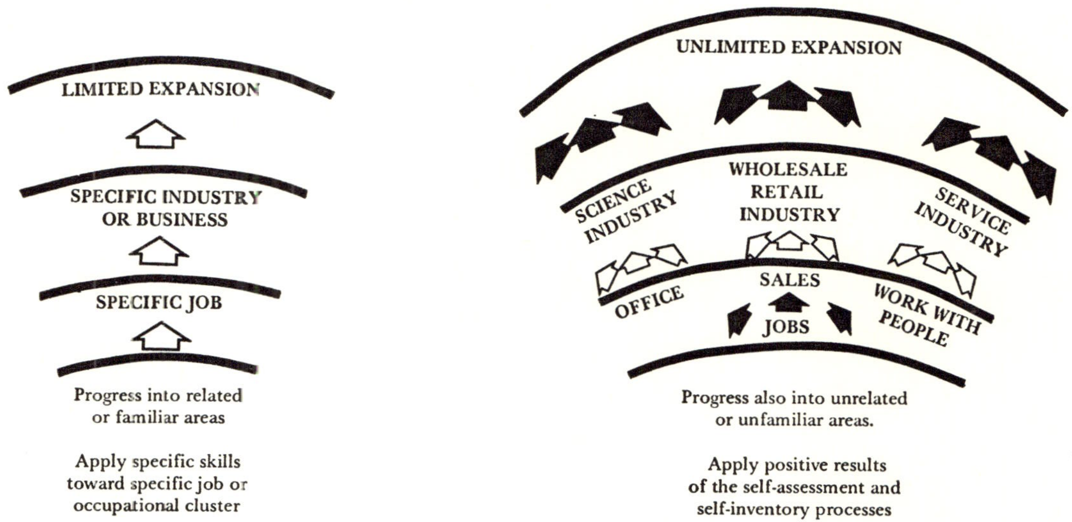

important to utilize all your resources, and to apply yourself toward gaining entry into these occupations.

For example, a job seeker may have gained skills in clerical work but have been employed in only one or two specific industries or businesses. That job seeker should explore other businesses and industries and make an effort to apply skills and work potential to other fields such as science, law, medicine, manufacturing and others. While job titles may differ and cause jobs to appear to be unrelated, the skills and work potential can very well apply to many fields. Clerical needs cut across all businesses and industries. Find out about these needs common in all fields. Skills and work potential for stock clerks, drivers, trade, maintenance, researchers, and administrative personnel can also be applied to many businesses and industries and other occupations.

One point to remember is that new businesses, demands and technological changes create new jobs which can be sources worthwhile exploring and which can be sources for new jobs. Expansions in business and industry can also create new jobs.

If you are a college graduate or have attended an educational institution of higher learning and lack meaningful work experience, ask yourself, whatever your academic background:

What were the personal gains I made in the learning process?

Were some of the gains made in terms of reinforcement of the ability to think, analyze, and comprehend sundry subject matters?

Did I acquire the ability to research, organize, and write?

Did I acquire or develop the ability to think and apply myself in terms of "width", "breadth", "depth", and "substance"?

Did I also develop a sense of striving towards a desired end?

Could these acquisitions and developments be employed by me to direct my job search into many job areas?

Can I utilize all of my resources in a private enterprise or to free lance in a specialty?

The matter of persistence is a key factor in job attainment. People and students are advised to apply for jobs consistently and to utilize all available resources in order to be more successful in the job search. One or two attempts at a job search and prolonged waiting for telephone calls or responses from employers or hiring or referral agencies are inadequate and will not land the job. Viewed realistically, for most, a few job search attempts is almost meaningless and will most likely not produce positive results.

Discouragement may most likely result after several or more attempts, but this critical stage can be overcome by being organized, persistent and by maintaining a positive outlook. Apply yourself totally until you are gainfully employed. Some frustration and discouragement are expected elements in job searching. The job seeker must accept this fact and realize that consistent application of total worthiness in the job search will eventually bring its reward, a desired job - or a job that gives you some satisfaction. Whatever happens in your job searching attempts, do not sell yourself short.

CHAPTER 6

COMMUNICATION CHANNELS OF THE WORLD OF WORK

"Defined positively, communication is a process which men practice when they seek a specific response from other people."[1] Here, communication avenues of the world of work concern themselves with the means by which you can communicate with prospective employers to seek positive responses. The various means employed by you can be categorized in numerous ways, but the important point to remember is that the most positive and effective means should be utilized whereby your interests will be best served. In other words, use the "best and most effective" method by which you can gain entry into jobs. For examples of various aspects of the communication process, see Chart 8, page 89.

Channels of communication with, and accesses to, employers vary. The process by whatever means, involves a sender and a receiver and the substance, impact and potential effect of communication are important, if not critical, to the process of job seeking. While some of the methods to be discussed are standardized and normally expected by employers, some approaches depend upon you and other factors and situations.

CHART 8

COMMUNICATION CHANNELS OF THE WORLD OF WORK

The following is an outline of some of the methods used by job seekers to communicate with and to establish positive relations with employers relative to job hunting. Channels of communication and access to employers vary. While some of these methods used are standardized and normally expected, some approaches utilized depend upon the job seekers and their personal sense of individual tastes, needs, desires, attitudes, behavioral patterns, lifestyles, sense of morality, and other values.

SECOND PARTY COMMUNICATION (when someone else speaks for you)
- Family influence
- Friends' influence
- Teachers, clergy, probation officers, and counselors
- Political influence (legislators, administrators, public officials, company officials, personnel employees, and others)
- Members of community associations, unions, fraternities, sororities, clubs, churches, and others

PERSONAL COMMUNICATION
- Written communication:
  - Letters of job inquiry
  - Letters of application
  - Applications
  - Follow-up letters to applications
  - Resumes
  - Self-inventories
  - References
  - Commendations, achievements, accomplishments, and others
  - Samples of written works, publications, and others

Credentials, certificates, degrees, licenses, and others
Photographs

Personal contacts:
Social, business, political, cultural, union, educational, religious, and others
Gratuities, personal favors, gifts, and others

Verbal or oral communication:
Tone of voice, use of words, volume, manner of greeting, and others

Non-Verbal communication: (body or physical language)

Affective factors: attitude, sincerity, interest, enthusiasm, confidence, and others

PERSONAL COMMUNICATION WITH EMPLOYERS

Personal communication with employers involves exactly just that – any means employed directed to employers by you to establish positive job contacts. The process involved and means utilized, relating to the recognition and awareness of you prior to actual interviews, can be an important phase. In fact, such initial points of contact with employers is deemed to be the first phase of the job interview.

Please note:

As will be explained again in this Chapter, employers cannot request information from you which makes reference to your race, sex, age, birthdate, birthplace, color, ancestry, parent's birthplace, ethnic background, physical characteristics, physical/mental handicaps, arrest or court record, names and addresses of relatives, associations or organizations to which you belong, and other personal data.[2]

Take note here that this is information which you willingly give to employers. The sample letters and resumes which you will review and which make reference to personal data submitted are provided only as examples and as illustrations.

WRITTEN COMMUNICATION TO EMPLOYERS

More extensive than usual, written submissions of letters, resumes, and other documents will eventually have to be submitted by you when jobs become more competitive and especially when prime or higher level jobs are advertised.

Written materials submitted to employers need not be elaborate, but this depends on your taste. Whatever style you select, the point to remember is to submit materials which are neat and easy to understand. Seek assistance if needed in writing and in reviewing the materials.

Letters of Job Inquiry:

These letters can be employed as initial points of contact with employers when you are uncertain as to whether job vacancies exist. Letters should not be sent at random but should be used selectively, based upon your interests and the type of business receiving your letters.

As an example, if you desire accounting type work, direct such letters to CPA and accounting firms; including offices within larger establishments which utilize accounting employees. Feel free to send many letters to selected firms while actively job seeking. (see Sample Letter of Job Inquiry, on page 92.)

Remember these points when transmitting these letters:

- Be brief
- Try to fill a need
- Try to arouse some kind of employer interest in your qualification and skills
- Request a response from the employer

Also, remember that employee benefits and other conditions of work can be discussed in interviews. Avoid mentioning these in your letters. You may, if you wish, also send a resume of yourself and follow-up with at least a telephone call if you feel this contact can prove to be helpful.

SAMPLE LETTER OF JOB INQUIRY

(date)

TO: (name of person, or personnel office)
(name of firm or company)
(address – street, city, state and zip code)

Dear :

I am interested in working for a Certified Public Accountant. It is my understanding that a C.P.A. firm such as yours is a most suitable place to seek satisfying and rewarding employment.

I am a graduate of Leeward Community College and majored in the Two-Year Accounting Program. I have also had previous work experience. I am willing to be considered for one of your beginning accounting or other related positions and have the desire to work in this field. I believe that I have suitable work traits, potentials and qualifications to meet with your expectations, and I believe that I can contribute to your company's productivity and growth.

Enclosed is a personal resume which includes my personal history, educational and work experience background, personal and community interests, and pertinent personal references. I am interested in being a part of your firm and would appreciate the opportunity to discuss my desire, qualifications and work potential with you. May I have an interview? I shall be glad to call on you at your earliest convenience.

Very truly yours,

(your signature)

(type your name)
(your mailing address)
(your telephone number)

Letters of Application:

Letters of application can be used when you are aware of specific job vacancies and feel that you qualify, or potentially can qualify. Direct your letters to this effect. These letters should not be sent out randomly, but sent to selected firms where vacancies are known to exist. Apply for as many job vacancies as you wish and include your resume.

Similarly, these letters should be brief, attempt to fill a need, should be interesting and should request responses leading to job interviews. Other matters relating to conditions of employment such as wages, fringe benefits, and hours of work can be discussed in interviews. Avoid mentioning these subjects.

Follow-up by telephone and request for interviews.

SAMPLE LETTER OF APPLICATION

(date)

TO: (name of person, or personnel office)
(name of firm or company)
(address – street, city, state and zip code)

Dear :

I am interested in working for a large hotel and I understand that a secretarial position is available. I also understand that a hotel chain firm such as yours is a most suitable place to seek satisfying and rewarding employment.

I am a graduate of Leeward Community College and majored in the Two-Year Secretarial Science Program. I am certified as being able to type 70 words per minute and to take dictation at a rate of 115 words per minute. I am well versed in office procedures and can operate most office machines and equipment. I believe that I possess suitable work traits, work potential and qualifications to meet the requirements of the secretarial position. I believe that I can contribute to your company's productivity and growth.

Enclosed is my resume which includes my history, educational background, personal and community interests, references, and proficiency certificates. I am interested in being a part of your hotel staff and would appreciate the opportunity to discuss my desire, qualifications and work potential with you.

May I have an interview? I shall be glad to call on you at your earliest convenience.

Sincerely,

(your signature)

(type your name)
(your mailing address)
(your telephone number)

Application Forms:

If other contacts have not been made, applications for employment can be considered to be the initial contact with employers. The purpose of application forms is to provide employers with as much information as possible about yourself. Personal data, educational background, work experiences, skills, special training, interests, involvements and personal references are usually asked. Application forms differ from firm to firm and from institution to institution, but basic personal data questions are asked. The important points to remember about filling out these forms are that applications should be:

Neat and readable:

Print or use a typewriter. Employers want to read materials which are legible.

Do not leave blank spaces on application forms:

Write in something as "don't know", "not applicable (N/A)", "a dash", or something positive or neutral.

As to past employment records and dates which you may have forgotten, guess as to year or month. In writing a narrative about your work experience or education and training, use the past tense of the verb such as "typed", instead of "I did typing", or "types."

While answering certain types of questions such as work experience or special training received and you find you need more space, do not hesitate to use a separate sheet of paper. Of course, if a copy of a resume is available, attach a copy of this to the application.

By State Law, employers may not request the following types of information from you:[3]

Race
Sex
Age, including birthdate
Color
Ancestry, as place of birth, birth place of parents, and ethnic background
Religion
Marital status, including courtesy titles as miss, mister and maiden name
Physical characteristics, as height, weight and size
Physical or mental handicaps
Arrest or court record
Organizations, associations, clubs, societies, lodges and others which you belong to
Name and address of relatives
Request photograph before hiring
Non-job related military experience; and others

Employers have a right to ask questions or request information pertinent to the requirements of the position, provided that such questions do not solicit information which can be used for discriminatory purposes.

Whenever these questions are asked, you can if you so desire, voluntarily answer. Certain personal data provided on other documents or materials transmitted to employers are also submitted voluntarily. Personal data questions are still asked on application forms, but seemingly, with the more established firms, these could be considered to be oversights rather than intentional.

Follow-up Letters to Applications:

After applications are submitted, follow-up letters can be sent to employers, after a reasonable time, perhaps after a week or so. (See sample Follow-Up Letter to Application, page 97). Follow-ups can be made on letters of job inquiry, letters of application, and application forms.

Follow-ups can also be made by telephone. Whatever means are employed, be pleasant and make an effort not to turn off employers. Just simply ask:

1) Whether your application was received and reviewed
2) Whether the job has been filled (or if potential openings exist), and then
3) Ask for an interview if the employer is still considering applicants

Follow-up letters to applications submitted to civil service agencies are not necessary. As a matter of procedure, the civil service agencies routinely respond to applications submitted and examinations administered.

Follow-up thank you letters can also be sent to employers after job interviews. This simple gesture could be appreciated.

SAMPLE FOLLOW-UP LETTER TO APPLICATION

(date)

TO: (name of person, or personnel office)
(name of firm or company)
(address - street, city, state and zip code)

Dear :

Recently I submitted a letter specifying interest in being employed by your firm. I hope that you have received and reviewed my application. (if appropriate) I applied for position. As I explained, I believe that I can contribute to your company's productivity and growth.

I am hoping that the position has not been filled. Or, if a similar position is open, I will be more than glad to discuss my desire to be a part of your firm and to call on you at your earliest convenience.

May I have an interview?

Sincerely,

(your signature)

(type your name)
(your mailing address)
(your telephone number)

Resumes:

A resume is a document which presents the most positive image of yourself to employers. In concise but meaningful terms, you can utilize a simple format to submit resumes to employers. Depending on your work experiences and other factors, resumes can be more than one or two pages in some cases. (See seven sample resumes of different ages and both sexes on pages 98 – 108.) *Take note that the personal data on these resumes are for sample and illustration purposes only.* Personal data on resumes and other materials transmitted by you to employers are to be submitted by you knowingly and voluntarily. It is your choice.

Other formats can be used, but the important thing is to list those matters and personal attributes which can be related to the jobs or potential positions applied. Refrain from flowery or too general phrases. Be specific in your statements. Mention your duties and responsibilities as well as other salient aspects of your employment.

As a matter of accepted practice, the current or last employment is listed first followed by other previous employment. And as has been mentioned, when describing the duties of previous employment and other activities, use the past tense of a verb as will be noted in the sample resumes.

SAMPLE RESUME 1

Your Name
Address
Telephone

Personal*	Single - Responsible and Reliable - 21 Years Old
Professional Objective	Private Secretary. Ultimate goal: Administrative Secretary for a large firm.

*Optional

Education	A.S. Degree; 1975 Leeward Community College Major: Secretarial Science; Two-Year Program Special emphasis in typing (65 wpm), shorthand (120 wpm), payroll, office equipment such as Monroe Calculator, Zerox, duplicating machine, and use of telephone.
Work Experience 1972 to 1974	Moana & Company, Honolulu, Hawaii. Perfume Wholesaler. Worked as part-time clerk - 4 hours a day, 3 times a week. Answered telephone, took messages, typed prices on labels, swept floor.
Summer Work 1971 to 1972	Worked as a trimmer at a local pineapple cannery for two summers to save money for college.
Volunteer Work 1971	Anne's Hospital for the Aged. Volunteered as a Nurse Aide for six months. Fed patients, read to and wrote letters for them. Also mopped floors, cleared food and dishes, and ran errands.
Background*	Brought up in Nanakuli and attended public schools in this area. Involved with Community Association. Attend Church regularly.
Interests	Interested in outdoor activities such as swimming, volleyball, tennis, and the gentle art of boy watching.
Skills	List skills which you possess.
References	List a few references with names, addresses and telephones.

Your signature Date

---

*Optional

SAMPLE RESUME 2

Your name
Address
Telephone

Personal*	Single - 5' 7" - 170 Pounds - 27 Years Old
Professional Objective	Bank Manager. Ultimate goal: Officer of large bank.
Education	A.S. Degree, 1968 Leeward Community College Major: Accounting - Two Year Program; Minored in Psychology. Special emphasis in Financing and Merchandising; considerable work in accounting and Data Processing.
Experience	Elsie & Company, Honolulu, Hawaii. Retail shoe sales. Started as clerk. After six months, transferred to Waipahu Branch as Assistant Manager. Responsible for all display work, newspaper advertising, and sales promotion. This branch has annual volume of $50,000.00.
Summer Work	Earned 50% of total college expenses selling vacuum cleaners and cooking ware on commission for two summers. Worked as a hand-trucker at a local pineapple cannery for one summer. Also worked part-time selling cookware.
Military* Service	United States Army 1963 to 1966. Communications specialist. After graduation from high school, volunteered into the service. Spent most of my duties in Vietnam working as a communications and pacifications relations officer.

Background*	Brought up in the Koko Head area. Active in community affairs such as Junior Chamber of Commerce and active alumnus of Leeward Community College. Member of social fraternity. Have traveled extensively on business throughout the Neighbor Islands.
Interests*	Primarily interested in hiking - outdoor activities and conservation societies, e.g. Save the Turf Foundation and Girl Watcher's Society.
References	List a few references with names, addresses and telephones.

Your signature Date

*Optional

SAMPLE RESUME 3

Your name
Address
Telephone

Personal*	Married - 5'8" - 145 Pounds - 30 Years Old
Professional Objective	Retail Sales Manager. Ultimate goal - manager of major retail outlet for a large national chain.
Education	B.A., 1966 University of Hawaii. Major: Marketing (completed college in three years); Special emphasis in Retail Sales and Merchandising; considerable work in Accounting and Data Processing.
Experiences 1969 to 1971	Walter Bea's Department Store, Hilo, Hawaii. Assistant Manager. In charge of all advertising

	and copy layout for this large department store. Worked closely with all buyers in planning sales campaigns. Assisted manager in working out modernization plans for basement level. Have taken two trips to the mainland to assist in selecting mens' suits and shoes.
1968 to 1969	Jacqueline & Company, Honolulu, Hawaii. Retail men's clothing. Started as a clerk in the downtown branch. After six months, moved to Waianae outlet as Assistant Manager. Responsible for all display work, newspaper advertising, and sales promotion. This outlet had a gross annual volume of $20,000 when I was assigned here, and had a gross annual volume of $40,000 when I left.
Military* Service	United States Army, 1966 to 1968. Infantryman. Spent most of my duty in Vietnam as an infantryman.
Background*	Raised in Waialua, Oahu. Active in community affairs such as the Junior Chamber of Commerce and active alumnus of the University of Hawaii. Member of the Hawaii Wholesale and Retail Association. Wife is a graduate student in Public Administration. No children. Have traveled extensively throughout the western part of the mainland and Neighbor Islands.
Interests	Primarily interested in marathon racing. Never won, but always finished.
References	List a few references with names, addresses and telephones.

Your signature Date

*Optional

SAMPLE RESUME 4

	Your name Address Telephone
Personal*	Good Health - 5'8" - 120 Pounds - Reliable
Professional Objective	Buyer. Ultimate goal: Buyer for major retail department store chain.
Education	Leeward Community College, 1976, A.A. Degree. Special emphasis in Speech, English, Reading, and Sociology.
Experience 1966 to 1973	JoJo's Department Store, Honolulu, Hawaii. Employed as senior salesclerk in Women's Apparel Department. Checked all sales slips at the end of day. Supervised 3 salesclerks. Checked inventory 4 times a year. Also handled customers' complaints on occasions.
1959 to 1962	Lori Ann & Company, Honolulu, Hawaii. Retail Food Store. Started as office clerk in Waialua Branch. After six months, transferred to main town branch as a salesclerk. Responsible for sales of imported food products from the mainland, Orient and Europe. Handled cash register and money. Totaled cash receipts at the end of the day.
Background*	Born and raised in Waialua, Oahu. Active PTA member. Busy with raising four children. Children now grown and self sufficient.
Interests	Primarily interested in furthering education in merchandising and administration and am

	currently enrolled in evening courses. Will continue until I complete my B.A. requirements.
Skills	List skills as language, specialties and others.
References	List a few references with names, addresses and telephones.

Your signature Date

---

*Optional

SAMPLE RESUME 5

Your name
Address
Telephone

Personal*	Independent - 5'6" - Can work odd hours Mature - Good health . Willing to relocate
Professional Objective	Editor. Desire position editing written narratives of newspaper articles, news letters, journals, periodicals, copyright materials, magazines, books and other literary works of a non-technical nature.
Education	University of Greater Learning, B.A. in English, 1960, Kaaholawe, Hawaii. University of Greater Learning, Post Graduate work, 1962.
Experience 1971 to 1978	Snowy Mountain Book Review Club, Honokaa, Hawaii. Book Reviewer. Reviewed recommended readings for club members and wrote objective reviews on books read. Rated books on a scale of one-to-ten. Books reviewed were

	non-fictional and fiction. Supervised three assistant reviewers.
1965 to 1970	Volcano Publishing Company, Hilo, Hawaii. Assistant Editor. Assisted in the review of manuscripts submitted for publication. Reviewed materials for grammatical errors, spelling, inconsistencies, redundancies, format and submitted these to the Chief Editor. Reviewed materials mostly of a non-technical nature such as novels, fiction, true to life stories, confessions, detective stories, love stories and the whole ball of wax which writers submit under their names or pseudonyms.
1962 to 1964	Clerk-typist. Typed manuscripts, correspondence, billings, and other written materials. Also typed inter and intra office memos and labels for the file system. Filed incoming and outgoing correspondence and answered telephone and took messages.
Interests	Have read about four to five books per week for the past fifteen years. Have kept current with contemporary fiction and non-fiction publications. Hike on occasion.
Association*	Member of the Club for Avid Readers for fifteen years.
Skills	Can read, write, speak and understand Spanish and French.
References	List a few references with names, addresses and telephones.

Your signature Date

*Optional

SAMPLE RESUME 6

Your name
Address
Telephone

Personal*	Married - 5'4" - 160 Pounds - Good Health
Employment Objective	Maintenance work for a large hotel.
Education	High School Graduate, 1968.
Experience 1975 to 1978	Darleen Shell Company, Honolulu, Hawaii. Maintenance man. Installed, tested, repaired and maintained all equipment and machinery within the premises such as small drill presses, vacuum cleaners, polishers and sanders. Also repaired and maintained sinks, water closets, and drains including piping systems and air conditioning units. Ordered parts for equipment and machinery. Have knowledge of and have used all types of tools and equipment in repair and maintenance work such as electric drills, household tools, sanders, wrenches, dies, electric voltage testing equipment, and other tools used in plumbing and electrical work.
1971 to 1975	The Unique Trucking Company, Honolulu, Hawaii. Truck driver. Loaded and delivered various types of merchandise - light and heavy. Drove a flat bed truck and large van to deliver merchandise.
1968 to 1971	Employed by various companies as a warehouseman, stock clerk, plumber's helper, maintenance man, laborer, and truck helper.

References — List references with names, addresses and telephones.

I can also provide references from previous employers attesting to my reliability and satisfactory work performed.

Your signature Date

---

*Optional

SAMPLE RESUME 7

Your name
Address
Telephone

Personal* — Widowed - Good Health - 5'7" - 130 pounds Outgoing

Employment Objective — Sales work in hardware outlet - wholesale or retail. Familiar with all types of automotive and electrical tools and parts.

Education — Sandwich Island College for Women. Earned a Bachelors Degree in Economics. Editor for College Newspaper, "The Liberation," for two years.

Experience

1967 to 1978 — Bonnie Hardware Company, Ewa Beach, Hawaii. Secretary to the manager. Took dictation, transcribed, typed final copies of correspondence. Also was charged with the supervision of two clerical help in the office. Responsible for the billing to customers, interviewing customers for credit application, receipt of payments, and recording of purchase transactions.

	Also verified financial stability of credit customers and purchased office equipment and supplies.
1952 to 1967	Initially employed as a clerk-typist and sales clerk. Typed, filed and recorded all incoming and outgoing correspondence for the company and also performed as a sales clerk at the counter and handled cash and credit transactions for customer purchases.
Background* and Interests and Involvement	Have resided in Ewa Beach for thirty years. Have been an active member of the Beach Club Association as President, Treasurer, and as a member for twenty years. Have also volunteered to work with juvenile delinquents who reside in the community. Assisted in forming the Neighborhood Fixit Club to help members of the community repair simple to complex mechanical and electrical appliances, home equipment and recreational equipment. Have also been a regular "door to door" solicitor for the Aloha United Way. Am still involved in volunteer activities for my church.
References	List some references with names, addresses and telephones.

Your signature Date

*Optional

Self Inventory:

The results of your self-inventory on work experiences and non-related employment, life's experiences, can be utilized either by incorporating it into the resume, or by submitting it as a separate document along with the resume.

Extract portions of the civilian and military work experiences inventoried, and utilize them if such assets can be related to the jobs you are applying for. As a matter of review, these categories of work experiences inventoried are:

Qualifications
Skills
Abilities
Knowledge gained
Work potential gained

Ask yourself, what assets can be extracted from these categories and used in your resume?

Extract portions of your self-inventory on positive past life experiences and utilize these assets if they can be related to the jobs you are applying for. Such life experiences are in the following areas:

Membership in clubs, associations and other organizations (in all areas of social, business, political, educational, recreational, military, domestic and religious)
Licenses, certificates, degrees earned (in all areas)
Specific activities and involvements (in all areas)
Specific achievements and accomplishments (in all areas)

Ask yourself, what aspects of these past life experiences can be extracted and utilized as part of your resume?

Positive aspects of the results of the self-assessment of your personal characteristics can also be employed in your resume.

References:

Personal references, by names or letters of recommendations, are requested of job applicants to verify past work experiences, stability and other facets which employers want to know about. Employers want to know something about job seekers over and above data previously submitted, especially when jobs being applied for require greater responsibilities. But for whatever general or specific reason, you will find it prudent to first ask permission before listing names as references, or in soliciting written references which reflect upon work history, personal character, responsibility, maturity and other positive assets. Do not take these for granted. You should not seek out references from a single source such as only from teachers, or all from friends. Choose one of each, but if possible, seek out references from various sources, references which can help attest to specific assets, such as reliability, honesty and stability. A good reference source is from past employers who have been satisfied with your work performance and have recognized your abilities and responsibilities.

If you do not have work experience or if you have had a prolonged absence from the work force or from society, select your references carefully. Ask people who can wisely satisfy employer's queries about you to be your job references.

There is no established required number of references, but if certain jobs call for honesty on the job because of handling or working with cash or other valuable merchandise, there is no reason why you should not request and submit more than one letter of recommendation attesting to this one asset.

Other Documents:

Other documents, such as commendations, achievements, samples of written works, publications, accomplishments, credentials, certificates, degrees, licenses, photographs, and others, written or earned, can be employed to enhance your chances. These should be utilized discriminately unless requested, or if you feel that submission of these materials will improve your chances. For example, even if you are applying for a clerical job, submission of an earned "Standard First Aid and Safety Certificate" will most probably enhance your job chances. Submission of your photograph is voluntary. Employers cannot "encourage" or request photos before you are hired.

PERSONAL/VERBAL CONTACTS WITH EMPLOYERS

Personal Job Interviews:

Initial personal contacts are normally made in job interviews. This phase of personal contact is an important part of establishing positive relations with prospective employers, and this aspect will be covered more extensively in another chapter.

Personal Favors and Gratuities:

As stated earlier, "the job seeker can utilize whatever initiative and means deemed best in a given situation."

In other endeavors, as in politics or in business, some exercise various means to achieve a given result. You as a job seeker can utilize personal contacts other than in job interviews to establish relations with employers. These contacts can be achieved through secretaries, gifts, gratuities, and other personal favors. Inviting potential employers to lunch, dinner parties, or establishing other types of contacts or rapport, can result in cementing closer relationships. These practices are not unknown.

While buttering-up employers or their representatives can potentially bear fruit, conversely, such practices can potentially backfire. But these are means which can be employed. As has been discussed, the job seeker can utilize whatever initiative and means deemed best in a given situation.

Non-Verbal, Physical or Behavioral Communication:

Non-verbal communication, body language, can contribute to positive or non-positive effects in job interviews, whether consciously or unconsciously practiced. The employers will feel, sense and react to the silent physical or behavioral communication aspects you project in job interviews.

As an example, "facial expressions frequently convey the speaker's attitudes. . . .,"[4] and "in essence, the speaker reflects facial expressions which complement and reinforce his message. . . ."[5] While you cannot be fully conscious of your facial expressions in job interviews, you should be aware that such expressions can and do affect employers. A ready smile here and there during interviews can be enhancing and to your advantage.

And as "in the majority of daily experiences, the friendly smile and eyes complement most messages."[6] Likewise in job interviews, friendliness helps to establish a more suitable environment, and is hard to beat. While hostility, unfriendliness and aloofness can be much easier to reject, employers may find it more difficult to reject friendliness.

"A speaker achieves maximum effectiveness in delivering his message when he looks at the person he is addressing. Eye contact, integral to delivery, serves as a speaker's method of communicating. . . ."[7] On the other hand, "when a listener maintains regular eye contact with the speaker, implicitly he is telling the speaker, I care, I want to hear what you have to say."[8]

Eyes carry various types of messages. As an example, how often have you held conversations with people, other than friends, and walked away with some kind of feeling that the eyes of the other people were either cold, angry, hostile, patronizing, sad, pleading, friendly, or wonderful, even though the color of the eyes were forgotten?

Employers may most probably have the same kind of feeling about you during and after interviews based on your eyes, facial expressions and other interrelated expressions.

Prolonged staring, whether conscious or unconscious, will most probably result in a non-positive effect. So will not looking at the employer or interviewer during job interviews.

As "natural, spontaneous and descriptive hand gestures strengthen delivery"[9] and "reinforce the speaker's message,"[10] so do other body movements and mannerisms.

While overplaying or overextending yourself in job interviews can have a non-positive effect, so can sitting in a stiff or awkward posture.

"To be yourself" is an easy bit of advice to give to a job seeker, but what of in the case of a job seeker who is either too demonstrative or too immobile? Or of a job seeker who projects undesirable mannerisms in job interviews? Or of a job seeker who reacts or behaves timidly, or too aggressively? Or of a job seeker who does not maintain normal eye contact with the employer?

Thus, "to be yourself" may not be the most beneficial advice to give for some.

Practice sitting as if you were in an interview, and when in doubt, use a minimum of gestures. Consult with others if need be.

As Chart 9, page 114 indicates, there are a variety of non-verbal, physical factors which job seekers should be aware of. Other aspects of non-verbal communication are also indicated.

Individual preferences may be directed towards utilization of only a few basics as the smile or simple hand gesture, but whatever, take care that conscious or unconscious use of other physical mannerisms does not jeopardize the outcome of job interviews.

SECOND PARTY COMMUNICATION

This method of communication is defined as being a situation when someone else speaks in the job seeker's behalf.

You, as a job seeker, may seek out the various sources for assistance and influences in obtaining jobs:

- Family and relatives
- Friends and acquaintances
- Teachers, members of the clergy, probation officers, counselors and other human services personnel
- Legislators, administrators, public officials, company officials, personnel employees, and others

CHART 9

NON-VERBAL COMMUNICATION

The following illustrates some of the non-verbal factors which have some positive or non-positive effect in the job search and in job interviews. Non-verbal communication, while only a part of the total communicative process to and with employers, does have a reactive effect on employers or interviewers.

Physical or Behavioral Communication (body language)

Appearance
Attire
Grooming
Walking
Standing
Poise
Sitting posture
Crossing arms
Physical gestures
Nervousness
Facial expressions - smile, frown, grimace and others
Eyes' expression - glare, hostility, friendly, sad, cold, patronizing, wonderful and others
Fidgeting, squirming, constant movements and others
Mannerisms
Greeting people - shaking hands, waving, patting and others

Presence of a Second Party

Affective Factors

Attitude
Sincerity
Interest
Enthusiasm
Confidence
And others

Written Communication

Letters of job inquiry
Letters of application
Applications
Follow-up letters to applications
Resumes
Self-inventories
References
Commendations, achievements, accomplishments and others
Samples of written works, publications and others
Credentials, certificates, degrees, licenses and others
Photographs

Members of community associations, unions, fraternities, sororities, clubs, churches, professional organizations, community service agencies, cultural associations and others

The sources mentioned above have already been discussed in the Chapter on Job Sources, and these are potential and viable sources which you can seek out and utilize. The listing of these sources does not mean that assistance is automatic or easy, but is given as a reminder that such sources do exist and can be of assistance.

Whatever means or combination of means employed by you in your quest for jobs, the results achieved should be foremost. You will remember that the U.S. Department of Labor survey indicated that "asking friends about jobs" was the second top ranking successful method used by job seekers and that another effective method used by job seekers was also in "asking relatives about jobs where they work."

CHAPTER 7

PERSONAL JOB INTERVIEWS AND PREPARATIONS FOR MEN AND WOMEN (HOW AND WHY)

A job interview is an important phase of job hunting. Generally for most people, this could be the crucial moment when prospective employers or interviewers make decisions on whether to hire you or recommend that you not be hired. The applications and resumes which you have submitted reveal only a part of you to employers. A personal job interview will reveal to employers other facets of you, face to face. So, potentially, the favorable impression that you make upon employers in personal interviews may be the deciding factor in getting jobs.

Subjectivity should be minimized in job interviews, but since employers or interviewers are human, they may in some cases have pre-conceived notions about you based on your application, resume, background, personal description, and other factors — even prior to interviewing you and acknowledging your employment background and qualifications. And realistically, while some interviewers or employers will have ingrained attitudes about people, some will be more liberal. If conditions are favorable, you are indeed fortunate. If not, do not be discouraged.

How you approach employers, how you conduct yourself during job interviews, how you appear to employers, and how you follow-up on interviews can influence the employer's positive thinking about you and in turn could be a deciding factor in obtaining jobs.

Common sense, circumstance, and above all sincerity in job seeking will dictate the course of action you take in pursuing and preparing yourself for job interviews. This depends on your individual situation, attitudes, and other factors.

To be discussed will be the how and why of preparation for and of interviews such as appearance, dress, inquiries, attitudes, conduct, reactions, things to do, and other aspects of job interviews. Some of the subjects under discussion will be sensitive in nature and possibly disapproving, superfluous and even amusing to some; but whatever views or reactions the job seeker may have on the following subjects, suggestions and comments, take these for what they are worth to you. These are worthy of review.

SOME PRELIMINARY PREPARATIONS

Depending on the type of job lead you are pursuing, it is a good practice to call and arrange for appointments – especially with private business firms. For a large firm or governmental agency, you can probably seek out the personnel office without appointments and fill out applications. The larger private establishments usually retain personnel to receive and interview job applicants.

If it is a small business firm and you are seeking a job without making an appointment, seek out the owner, manager or the key person who interviews and hires. If at that time your presence seems like an intrusion, apologize and make arrangements for an interview.

If you will note, help wanted ads usually specify whether to call first, to send a resume, or to just walk in and apply. It will be prudent to follow these directions.

When you have time, and especially if you are a newcomer to Hawaii, obtain a Hawaii State Driver's License. You can also obtain a State Identification Card. Also try to establish a permanent or stable residence address. You can obtain permission to use a friend's or relative's address as a mailing address for yourself. Avoid using a general delivery address. If you have funds, open a checking or savings account. Credit stability may be checked. These things will help you in your job hunt as these possessions may ease the employer's mind as to your stability and permanency within the community.

One important preparation to remember is to prepare for and seek jobs well in advance of your need.

PERSONAL HYGIENE

Attention to one's personal hygiene is deemed to be an important aspect of job hunting. But adherence to irregular, normal or meticulous personal hygiene depends on the job seeker's personal situation, attitude, lifestyle, and the type of job being sought.

With regard to personal hygiene, this is basic for both men and women. Be clean and neat. Bathe or shower if needed. Especially in warm weather, if you have been perspiring profusely prior to a job interview and you have the time and access to a bathroom or shower, cleanse yourself again. Use a deodorant if needed. If not, do the best you can.

Depending on the interview time, brush your teeth or rinse your mouth again. Gargle with a mouthwash if needed. If this is not possible, do whatever you can to freshen yourself. There are mouth fresheners which can be carried around.

WOMEN

Many women and young ladies may choose not to use make-up, but for those of you that do, here are some tips on grooming and care. Preferences will vary, but again use your judgment or seek advice.

If you use lipstick, apply a natural looking red or pink neutral lipstick shade; and use just a slight amount of base make-up – what you would wear by streetlight.

If you use false eyelashes, use the nice fringy natural ones. Lay off those hedge-rows that bat madly every time you look up or blink your eyes.

If you use eye shadow that is less than conservative, use a normal color.

Eyes are beautiful. Enhance them. Maximize their appearance to your advantage. They can speak volumes for you.

Use a little perfume or cologne, but no overpowering scents. Save this for your heavy dates. Something discreet or flowery is preferable.

Manicure your nails and use a conservative color or clear nail polish.

Hairstyles vary from year to year, and however hair is set, groom and arrange hair in an attractive neat style that is face-contouring, becoming and flattering to you. Many hairstyles are worn or fashioned naturally, and this is becoming. If possible, avoid extreme styles until you have reconnoitered the job situation. After you have been hired, then, if it is your desire, stylish or even casual hair-dos can evolve.

As to what may be unsightly hair to some employers, remove any hair on your legs and under your arms, especially if these are visible during interviews. For many women and young ladies, this is taken for granted.

With respect to clothing, you should wear becoming and discreet clothing for initial interviews. During or after interviews, you may notice that the ladies that work in the office or place of employment are not so conservative or so discreet. Some may wear extreme or casual clothing on the job. But for that first interview, be conservative and use your good judgment.

A fitted dress, a skirt and blouse, or a simple suit are in good taste. Depending on the situation and style of the day, neat and matching pants suits may be permissible.

Generally muumuus and casual attire should not be worn to job interviews. Neither should tank tops, halters, cut offs, tube tops, sun dresses, bare backs, shorts, T-shirts, sweaters and other too casual wearing apparel.

And while the times of the day call for that "braless look", it will be prudent to wear a brassiere, especially when wearing knit, too thin, close fitting, or loose hanging garments.

And while the climate and casualness of the Hawaiian atmosphere generously permit casual wear for many occasions and everyday wear, common sense and common courtesy, at least, should dictate being presentable for job interviews.

But again, as a reminder, personal situations, attitudes, the jobs and perhaps physical size and circumstance, will dictate what you will wear to job interviews.

Wear nylon stockings in a standard beige tone if you think this is right for your job. However, use your discretion as to shades and color.

Use appropriate shoes whether these be low to medium to high heeled shoes. Select a shoe style to match the clothes you wear. Do your best to look appropriate and nice.

Make sure your shoes are clean and polished if needed. Unless you have a foot ailment, stay away from slippers.

If you wear jewelry at all, make them small and simple or else wear one or two smart looking pieces. Good-looking costume jewelry will suffice adequately, but no more.

When in doubt about the amount of make-up, jewelry or clothing, do what models do at times; stand in front of the mirror, take off some make-up, jewelry and check how you look. Seek assistance from others, if needed.

Remember, your appearance and what you wear depend on the type of job you are applying for. It helps when you dress and groom yourself nicely. At any rate, you may not work in the clothing which you wear to the interview, but you might not get the job if your general appearance is not appropriate, neat or satisfactory to employers or interviewers.

MEN

Now for you men: Be clean shaven - if at all possible. If your personal circumstance leaves you without a razor, borrow one from anyone - even rent one from a barber.

If you sport a beard or mustache, do your best to look neat and sharp. A beard can be sharp and handsome looking, but not when it's straggly.

Comb your hair, and if possible, have a trim or haircut, if needed, before job hunting. Here, prospective employer's tastes and tolerance may differ as to style or length of hair, but under your personal circumstances, groom yourself as best you can. Use a wig if you have to.

Make sure your fingernails are clean and neatly trimmed.

As to clothing, wear conservative clothing when in doubt. If it is an office type, or sales or professional job you are applying for and if it's a large firm or institution, wear a coat and tie - at the least, a tie with your shirt. Wear a suit if you think it necessary, and if one is available. Mod fashions may be in style, but use your judgment. If at all possible, see what the other men in the office are wearing prior to the interview.

For a blue collar or non-professional job, whether it be a gas station attendant job to a stock clerk position, wear suitable pants and a clean shirt. Long sleeves look nice, but short sleeves are permissible and understandable in warm weather. If you think it will help, wear a tie. Unless you are just going through an exercise, stay away from shorts and too casual wear.

As to footwear, wear solid colored or conservative shoes - cleaned and shined. Certain types of two-toned footwear or sandals may be okay, but again, use your judgment. Unless you have a foot ailment, stay away from slippers. With respect to jewelry or other body ornaments, wearing too many may have non-positive reactions.

Again, you may not work in the clothing which you wear to interviews, but you might not get the job if your appearance is not appropriate, neat, or satisfactory to employers.

THE HANDICAPPED

For men and women who are unable to be impressively attired due to physical difficulties such as being confined in wheel chairs, or due to wearing of prosthetic devices or support equipment, or due to unusual physical structure, or due to lack of normal vision, do your best to look presentable. Whether or not there has been acceptance by individuals of the nature of their impairments, compensation through expansion of positive personality traits can offset attire inadequacies.

Since physiological or other factors may be the contributing cause to difficulties in communication or physical movements during job interviews, those with impairments need not be overly concerned about these. Employers may most likely understand if the nature of the impairment is obvious.

THE INTERVIEW

First impressions can be all important and here are suggestions – things to remember which will help both men and women to be more successful in job searches.

Get a good night's rest, or be sure that you are rested and are in a good frame of mind. If you are not up to it, cancel the appointment or job hunt as your best side may not show during interviews and could otherwise sabotage a good opportunity. If an interview time has been arranged, be prompt, even a little early.

If possible, know something about the company and job to which you are applying. You may be asked about the company or about the job.

Be prepared to answer difficult or problem questions such as "what are your goals?", or "why do you want to work for this company?", or "why do you think that you can do the job?" or "why should the company hire you over the other job applicants who are waiting in the other room?", and other similar type questions.

Ready answers are strongly advised in a case where a job seeker has had prolonged absences from the labor market or from society. Being long term unemployed may be due to such reasons as being in prison, being a ward of the State or private institution, experiencing prolonged absences due to illness or other similar confinements, having raised a family, and other unusual absences.

Depending on the interviews, "stress" techniques may be employed in interviews. This is where interviewers purposely ask questions or lead you into conversations which could possily startle or offend you. The reaction is then observed. Bear in mind that such an interview can happen to you.

Take a pen with you, as you may have need for one, and have the necessary documents and information ready. These would be your social security number, schooling, dates attended, certificates and degrees, references, employment history, military service records, alien registration cards, and others. Very likely these have already been included in the application form, but be accustomed to having them with you when job searching.

Also have a resume ready if you have not submitted one yet. If you are not sure about how to prepare one, seek help and learn to prepare one. It is wise to have one available, expecially if you have an extensive or special background, although some jobs may not require resumes.

Be prepared to take aptitude, proficiency, personality, and physical tests.

If you wear a hat or cap, remove it during the interview. Above all, remove any chip on your shoulder. Being unfriendly, aloof, or hostile will not help you at all. Also remove any non-positive judgment you may have about the employer. Try to have a positive attitude and an open mind.

When called in for the interview, greet the interviewer or employer by his or her last name. If you do not know their names, greet them by courtesy titles such as Ma'am or Sir.

Shake hands only if the interviewer offers his or hers.

Smile during the greeting, and if possible, during the interview. Practice if need be, for this will enhance your chances.

Remain standing until the interviewer invites you to be seated. Sit erect and properly. (Women should use their judgment in regard to what is modest and play it safe by sitting with both feet on the floor, especially when wearing skirts. Men should also be attentive to their sitting posture as not slouching or sitting in an unprofessional manner.)

Keep your hands in a relaxed position or folded on your lap. Do not clench your hands or cross your arms despite the temptation to do so. Also remain relaxed, even if you do not feel that way inside.

Look at the interviewer as you speak and do not look off into space or at the walls. Speak slowly and clearly. Do not run over yourself, or speak faster than you can think. Be careful of your manner of speech. You may not use the King's English, but it is *how* you speak that counts, because the manner in which you say things will reflect your feelings, attitudes, knowledge, capabilities and potential.

Also avoid localisms, slang, and hip talk.

"The human voice may be analyzed in terms of volume or projection, tone quality, pitch and rate of speaking."[1] While people are not really aware of their own voices at times, practice sessions will shed light on how their voices actually sound and are projected. These sessions will give some indication to job seekers of how others hear them. For the majority of job seekers, access to audio visual equipment would be difficult indeed, but should such equipment be readily available, practice interview sessions will allow job seekers to see and hear themselves reacting to various simulated interview situations.

But access to a mirror and a tape recorder should not be difficult. Using these tools, job seekers will still be able to see and hear themselves. Speaking into a tape recorder and listening to the play back will give job seekers some idea of how they sound to others. Improvement, if needed, can then be made. And why not take this one step further and practice answering questions? There should be no embarrassment or hesitation for jobs are at stake.

For individuals who anticipate or are enrolled in schools and colleges, taking courses in Interpersonal Communication and related subjects will enhance job seeking verbal and written and employment potential.

And during interviews, be attentive and respond quickly and briefly to questions. Answer questions completely and truthfully. Remember, the answers given must be consistent with the information contained in your application, resume or other material already submitted. Should employers hire, only to find out later that there were untruths, you will most likely be penalized later.

Ask questions when in doubt. This will indicate your interest as well as yout discriminating ability.

Mention your interests like volunteer work, hobbies, extra curricular activities, professional associations and others only if the interviewer asks. If you lack work experience, your volunteer and other community activities and special interest may put you in a favorable light with employers.

Some reasons for inquiry into your non-employment activities are to find out about your involvement in various types of activities, to find out about your likes and interests, as well as to find out about your personal incentive and consideration to give time and energy without compensation. While some non-employment activities may be frowned upon by employers, usually those activities which are meaningful, constructive and unselfish in nature are looked upon favorably by employers.

When the interview is concluded, thank the interviewer or employer for the interview, and politely leave.

First interviews are usually for screening purposes and getting to know you. A specific job offer may not be made at the time. The prospective employer is taking a reading of you. Remember, the employer, without mentioning it, may also be considering you for other positions in the company. At any rate, other applicants for this same job will also have to be considered. Remember, you will most likely be competing with others for the job.

You may be asked to call again or follow-up, but in any case, always follow-up by letter or a telephone call to express a continued interest in the job. You are not being pushy by doing this, but simply indicating your interest and your seriousness.

THINGS WHICH TURN EMPLOYERS OFF

During interviews, the employers or interviewers are observing you and what you say and do will make some kind of impression on them. Perhaps the following things should be discussed as a reminder of what not to do – or things which generally turn employers off.

Try not to make your first inquiry, "How much will I make?" Never say, "I desperately need a job", or "I can do anything," or "I will do anything." (This writer has often responded to the latter statement by lifting an eyebrow and then slowly asking, "Anything?" Whereupon the maker of the statement then had second thoughts about the statement made.) Employers want people who can do something specific or who possess work potential. Try to refrain from making statements you don't mean or are not sure about. Initial wage inquiries, desperation in job seeking, and meaningless statements can have non-positive effects.

Avoid wearing dark glasses - unless for health, vision or other legitimate reasons. You have nothing to hide, and besides, employers want to look at you. Wearing dark or sun glasses can potentially cause a non-positive effect.

Do not wear slippers, again unless for health reasons. If you have to, explain that it is only a temporary ailment. And forget wearing too casual attire or shorts.

If you are thinking about going barefooted to job interviews, forget it.

Native costumes should not be worn to job interviews. But again, this depends on the type of job being sought. Seek advice on this matter from cultural peers who have experienced job interviews.

Do not chew gum, smoke, eat candy, or munch on anything. Employers may find these disconcerting.

Minimize signs of nervousness, such as drumming your fingernails on the desk or chair. Also avoid fidgeting and squirming, that is, if possible. Sometimes it is a temptation, but control yourself.

For young ladies and perhaps men, do not fuss with your hair or clothing. Self-consciousness will be evident.

Do not stare off into space or look at walls or ceilings. If you are shy or timid by nature, seek help and try to overcome this. Or practice looking at people by looking into a mirror and speaking to yourself.

In addition, do not clutter the interviewer's desk.

Try not to do all the talking or constantly interrupt the interviewer. Remember, that while aggressiveness is a trait which some employers desire in their employees, being overly aggressive or being more aggressive than interviewers may turn them off. Interviewers may feel that they want to control the situation in job interviews. Physical aggressiveness has a relationship to verbal aggressiveness, but being discussed is verbal aggressiveness. Remember, while the applicant may think so, the interviewer may not relate verbal aggressiveness as a sure sign of intelligence.

Let the interviewers lead the conversation and do not involve yourself in deep arguments during interviews. Disagreements are in order, but if you must, do so in a manner which will not offend interviewers.

Avoid making derogatory or bad mouth remarks about former employers or other people. Do not slander anyone, even if it is justifiable, as it is you who will be judged and not the absent party. You may be in the right, but it is going to reflect on you in an unpleasant or non-positive manner if you do. Unpleasant discussions should not take place during job interviews, but if the interviewer asks about a former employer, respond in a positive or neutral manner.

Do not mention personal matters, especially those involving family, money, health or other problems, unless asked. If interviewers or employers want to know about your personal life or your problems, they will ask.

Certain lifestyles may not be acceptable subjects to employers, so avoid mentioning them unless specifically asked. Keep in mind that certain lifestyles may be diametrically opposed to those of interviewers or employers you are in contact with.

And above all, do not bring friends or anyone else with you to the interview for moral support. This will be construed as a sign of immaturity and can cause a non-positive effect. However, if there is a problem in communicating with employers in the English language or if some other physical or mental disability prevents normal conversation and assistance is needed, the presence of the second party should be explained - preferably prior to the job interview.

A critique of you by friends in a job interview exercise can provide you with some idea of how employers might perceive you. Ask your friends to review your potential performance in job interviews. Use *Chart 10, Critique of Applicant in Job Interview,* page129, as a tool for an assessment of yourself. Have your friends assess you by checking off the proper qualitative categories on the right side of the Chart.

OVERVIEW

Thus far, the discussion has been on approaches, personal interview, general conduct, appearance and attitudes. The resumes and applications which you have submitted reveal only a part of you to employers. Your education, employment history, personal background, skills and other tangibles are pretty obvious. These can be substantiated through reference checks and testing. But during interviews, employers also want to know about the other facets of you — the what and how of you. In view of the previous discussion on employers in Chapter 2, ask yourself these questions:

Can I provide adequate explanations to my work potential?
Can I explain my work history in terms of what I did?
Can I provide answers to offset lack of work experience?
Can I describe my work skills?
Can I provide answers to non-positive factors in my life?

CHART 10

CRITIQUE OF APPLICANT IN JOB INTERVIEW

(name)
(individual being interviewed)

	Very good	Satisfactory	Fair - can be improved	Needs improvement	Comments
1. Initial or opening presentation in response to interviewer.					
2. General appearance - grooming (face and hair), makeup, beard, mustache, shave, cosmetics and others.					
3. Clothing - attire, dress, jewelry, neatness, appropriateness and others.					
4. Footwear.					
5. Sitting posture.					
6. Eye contact.					
7. Ability to describe past work experiences, education and/or training.					
8. Ability to explain "lack of qualifications" for job in terms of potential, positive personal traits, reliability, volunteer work and others.					
9. Ability to explain equipment, tools, machine, instruments, and other mechanical, electric or electronic aids used.					
10. Ability to explain skills, techniques, processes, procedures and other facets.					
11. Ability to explain personal goals, interests, desires and other related aspects.					
12. Ability to explain non-positive factors in personal life - disabilities, poor health, poor work record, poor personal record and prolonged absence from the work force.					
13. Ability to answer questions or make statements on job or company.					
14. Ability to respond and answer questions - accurately, sincerely, quickly and others.					
15. Aggressiveness (consider job applied for) - Too strong? Too much? Pushy?					
16. Shy? Bashful? Timid? Too reserved?					
17. Conversation or manner of speech - Audible? Understandable? Tone of voice?					
18. Physical mannerisms - Nervous? Fidgety? Distracting? Non-positive in nature?					
19. Overall enthusiasm?					
20. Overall attitude?					
21. Overall job interview performance?					

Do I agree that my positive characteristics can help to influence employers in job interviews?

If so, am I willing and can I demonstrate positive and potential assets during interviews?

Will my positive projection be adequate in interviews?

Can I really be myself in interviews? Or, is improvement or modification needed?

Am I what employers are looking for?

Some of you may not agree with some of the things which have been discussed, or these may be old stuff to you, but consider or reconsider their worth. These are practicalities and realities involved in job searching.

If you believe that "positive adjustment" for the purpose of job interviews is necessary in your situation and that this adjustment or modification will enhance your job chances, then reflect on this and take steps to make improvement. You are not being asked to change your personality, your cultural habits, your lifestyle or basic attitudes – whatever they may be. You are being advised to *modify* your approach, behavior and attitudes when you look for jobs. Remember, job seeking is a two-way street. By considering or hiring you, the employer is performing an act of faith and is willing to meet you halfway.

As a point to remember, while "being yourself" may be advantageous for some job seekers in job interviews, "being yourself" may be disadvantageous for others.

Looking for a job and being interviewed may not be an easy experience for you. Nor is it always easy to force yourself to hunt for jobs day after day and to follow-up on leads and interviews. But in order to achieve results you want, you will have to do things you do not want or like to do. People can help, but only to a certain extent. You must be willing to help yourself in order to achieve desired results. When you pound-the-pavement looking for jobs and face employers, you're on your own.

It is sincerely hoped that what has been discussed will help you to help yourself when you look for employment.

Keep applying for jobs. Work at it. If one prospective employer turns you down, keep your spirits up and contact as many more employers as you can. You have something to offer. With the tight labor market, it is going to be pretty competitive, but keep trying to find the job for which you qualify — or believe that you can do. That job exists somewhere. Remember, you are just as good and capable, if not potentially, as the next person.

CHAPTER 8

BARRIERS TO EMPLOYMENT

Barriers to employment do exist. Awareness of the wide range of barriers, or difficulties, can assist you as a job seeker when you encounter them. Being aware of potential difficulties will help you as a job seeker to anticipate, prepare, and strengthen your frame of mind and attitudes while job searching. You should analyze these difficulties, if known beforehand, and endeavor to resolve some, if not most, of them. It is realized that there are obstacles which exist prior to job hunting, as with personal problems or disabilities, but you will probably encounter obstacles which you are unaware of.

Some job searchers will be less fortunate than others in their job seeking. Depending on a variety of factors, some job applicants may encounter only minor difficulties or none at all, while others will encounter obstacles which may be very difficult to overcome. Hopefully, in the process of job searching, you will be able to overcome or minimize these difficulties.

BARRIERS OR OBSTACLES

What are these barriers in order that they can be identtified? Barriers to employment are numerous. Most of them fall within the range of personal, social, political, economic, cultural and religious aspects of the times. Various influences contribute to barriers. In more simple terms, these barriers arise due to the following realities:

People/community attitudes about people in general
Ethnic and cultural differences
Being a newcomer
Being overqualified
Lack of work experience
Lack of knowledge of the employment market
Shortage in certain types of jobs
Lack of self confidence
Inability to speak acceptable American English
Mental/physical/social disabilities
Lack of transportation
Lack of money for presentable clothes
Babysitting problems
Employer's expectations and requirements
Prolonged absences from the job market or from society
Work and environmental situations
Personal problems
Age
Sex
Appearance
And other numerous situations

However, one big barrier may be the job seeker. The job seeker may be unwilling to adjust to the community, to employer's expectations, and to other people. Also the job seeker may not be willing to accept different types of jobs and newer responsibilities, lesser paying jobs, less secure positions and other less favorable situations.

The following will present some observations on barriers to employment here in Hawaii.

ASSESSMENT OF BARRIERS BY THE HAWAII STATE DEPARTMENT OF LABOR AND INDUSTRIAL RELATIONS

In a *Manpower Review,* based on the first half of 1975, the Hawaii State Department of Labor and Industrial Relations listed these obstacles which reduced the employability of applicants seeking employment services through their offices:[1]

Overqualification

(which assumed increased importance as an employment barrier during the current tight labor market situation. As related aspects of this obstacle, most of the jobs available were generally low paying, with little security, unchallenging, and uninteresting.)

Age, too young

Age, too old

Inability to attain proper motivation and aspiration

Health problem

Personal problem

Child care problem

Care of other family members

Language as a barrier to employment was most apparent among recent Vietnamese immigrants*

In another publication, the State Labor Department assessed barriers to employment as being due to:[2]

Poor work attitudes

Lack of motivation

Lack of transportation for the economically disadvantaged

Lack of education and/or job skills (the major barrier to employment)

Discrimination

(Most common illegal criteria that employers sometime use):

Race

Physical handicap

Age

Arrest record

Lack of child care centers

*Many immigrant groups including Filipinos, Koreans, Samoans, Chinese and Japanese have problems with the English language, as do immigrant groups from the western and eastern hemispheres who settle on the mainland. But due to recency as a factor, the job seeking problems have been more prominent for the newest arrivals — as they will be for other incoming groups in the future in any locale.

- Health problems
  - Handicapped
  - Overweight
  - Physical and/or mental illness
- Personal problems
  - Lack of motivation
  - Alcoholism or drugs
- Care of family
  - Elderly person
  - Handicapped
- Garnishment

ANOTHER ASSESSMENT OF BARRIERS

During the spring of 1973, the author conducted a random sample survey of barriers to employment. Personal consultations, discussions in class and in various workshops brought to light certain difficulties encountered by people which varied, but with a series of factors which appeared with some regularity. Such regularity prompted this sample survey, the purpose of which was to ascertain specific difficulties students encountered when looking for work.

A rather simple questionnaire form was used. See Chart 11, page 136, for a revised form of the questionnaire. With the cooperation of instructors, classes in history, anthropology, English, and others were surveyed, as well as students who were roving around the campus. Two hundred and six (206) students were polled. The age, sex, ethnic backgound and status in life varied. Most of the students polled were at one time or another interviewed for jobs. The results of the sample survey are presented in Chart 12, page 137.

Random polling methods were used in producing these results and the sampling was rather limited. Thus, these results cannot be considered to be statistically valid, but students did express situations which they felt were barriers and which personally affected them in their search for jobs. Whether their expressions were based on facts or feelings, their beliefs still constituted barriers for them. The numbers in Chart 12 are

CHART 11

BARRIERS TO EMPLOYMENT

Barriers to employment are numerous. Most of them evolve from the personal, social, economic, political, cultural, and religious aspects of the times. Please list all the barriers or difficulties which you strongly feel affect you personally in your search for jobs. Individual returns will be held in confidence. Please list these difficulties by the order of importance, or order of most difficulty.

1.

2.

3.

4.

5.

6.

7.

8.

9.

10.

	YES	NO
Have you ever beeen interviewed for a job?	☐	☐
Have you ever been employed?	☐	☐
If employed did you find it easy to get your last job?	☐	☐
Were you qualified?	☐	☐
OPTIONAL		
Have you been in the Islands less than five years?	☐	☐
What is your sex?	_____	
What is your racial, ethnic background?	_____	
YOUR AGE RANGE		
Below 20 years?	☐	
Between 20 to 30?	☐	
Between 31 to 40?	☐	
Between 41 to 50?	☐	
Over 50 years?	☐	

CHART 12

A SURVEY OF BARRIERS TO EMPLOYMENT AS EXPRESSED BY 206 STUDENTS OF A TWO YEAR COMMUNITY COLLEGE

Barrier	Number
RACIAL FACTORS	
Ethnic background, race	66
Prejudice	19
Racial	13
Cultural	3
WORK, EXPERIENCE, SKILL FACTORS	
Lack of experience, skill, ability	73
Lack of work experience	20
No local experience	1
Unskilled	1
Lack of salesmanship	1
EDUCATIONAL FACTORS	
Lack of education	59
Too much education	5
Lack of credentials, certificates	4
Lack of college degree	1
GENERAL APPEARANCE FACTORS	
Personal appearance	41
Long hair, beard	11
Dress and grooming	9
Physical cleanliness	1
PERSONAL, POLITICAL, SOCIAL CONTACT FACTORS	
Lack of personal, political, social contacts or connections	34
Social life, background, associates	19
Lack of political influence	6
Relationship	2
Middle class status	2
Class	1
AGE FACTORS	
Too young or too old	41
PERSONAL TRAITS FACTORS	
Personal traits	10
Agressiveness	6
Attitude	5
Lack of confidence during job interviews	2
Impressions	1
Nervousness in job interview	1
Character	1
Lack of agressiveness	1
Lack of maturity	1
COMMUNICATION FACTORS	
Language barrier or difficulty	21
Grammar, speaking ability, verbal contact, speech	4
Speech patterns	3
JOBS, LABOR MARKET CONDITIONS	
Lack of availability of jobs	14
Lack of part-time jobs	4
Lack of knowledge of jobs, labor market	3
Shortage of desired jobs	2
Weekend-work	1
HEALTH FACTORS	
Physical Handicaps	12
Health	3
Illness	1
MARITAL STATUS	
Marital Status	2
Married	2
Divorced with children	1
FINANCIAL FACTORS	
Financial Status	11
Welfare	5
Lack of money for clothes	1
SEX	11
RELIGION	10
LACK OF TRANSPORTATION	7
NEW IN HAWAII, NON-RESIDENT, NOT U. S. CITIZEN	7
NO BARRIER	7
COMPETIVENESS	5
MILITARY OR DEPENDENT STATUS	5

Chart continued on next page.

LACK OF EXPERIENCE WITH PEOPLE 3
LACK OF DRIVER'S LICENSE 2
JOBS TOO FAR 2
NO INTERVIEW 2
INTERVIEWER'S BIASES 1
INTERVIEW SYSTEM. 1
SCREENING SYSTEM. 1
SENIORITY SYSTEM 1
ATTENDANCE. 1
LACK OF GOOD REFERENCES . . . 1
AUTOMATION. 1
TEST REQUIREMENT 1
TOO HIGH JOB ASPIRATION. 1
LACK OF AREA RESIDENCY. 1
APPLICATION FORMS NOT INDIVIDUALIZED. 1
HABITS 1
LAZINESS. 1
INABILITY TO FILL OUT FORMS . . 1
INTERVIEWER'S LACK OF CONCERN. 1
NO COMMENT 1

individual responses to a given situation, and the headings or categories by name were derived from grouping of similar or related responses or factor situations.

Two other small sample surveys taken in workshops revealed similar leading categories of barriers, or difficulties encountered. The groups in these polls consisted of counselors, teachers, housewives, professionals, clergy, and staff members of a Model Cities Program. There were mature and job experienced people in both groups.

A recent survey of a class* produced similar results as listed in Chart 12.

COMMENTARY

As can be observed from the assessments and expressions of job finding difficulties, some of the barriers seem to be relatively easy to overcome, while others seem to be very difficult to overcome. Some were personal in nature and others were beyond the individual's control. Some were, or seemed to be, discriminatory while others were not.

Should additional polls be taken, it is the feeling of this writer that such surveys will produce similar results, or expressions.

An oscillating relationship exists between the job finder and obstacles encountered. This relationship can be defined as a continuum ranging from mild to adverse difficulties which confront the job seeker and which have varying effects on the

*Survey taken December 2, 1976.

individual, depending on the individual and factors surrounding the employment situation. Perhaps one way of expressing this relation is to state that the stronger the adverse reaction to each barrier encountered by a job seeker, the greater the difficulty in overcoming the problem. And, conversely, the less adverse reaction to each barrier encountered, the greater the chances for minimizing or overcoming the barrier. And the degree of difficulty is dependent upon the individual job seeker, circumstance, competitiveness, the employer, influences exerted and other factors. When an adverse reaction to each barrier becomes greatly reduced, the greater the chances for successful job searches.

Hopefully, it is wished that the transitional process with its encumberances, from job seeking to being hired, will not be severe for you as a job seeker. As has been ascertained, however, you can expect to encounter difficulties. As best you can, individually or with assistance, endeavor to minimize or overcome difficulties encountered in your job search. You should exercise care in making judgments about whether job obstacles encountered are truly what they are or whether these difficulties are the result of personal feelings. There is a difference.

As part of your job searching, reflect on these barriers, or situations, for these are realities in any given community. Being born and raised in the Islands will not automatically provide you with an easy access to a job. Difficulties will still exist. But whatever the barriers may be, do not be discouraged. Analyze them and attempt to realistically resolve them. Should these barriers prove to be too difficult, seek advice and help if you need it. There are people sources, governmental agencies, special programs, your family and friends to help you. You are not alone. Most people care. Strive to overcome these barriers when encountered. Remember, you are just as good and capable, if not potentially, as the next job applicant. You have much to offer.

CHAPTER 9

EQUAL EMPLOYMENT OPPORTUNITY LAWS AND ENFORCEMENT AGENCIES WHICH ASSIST JOB SEEKERS

The term rights of an individual is a common and frequently used expression, and at times, due to emphasis and need, is reinforced and nourished to replenish the substance of its proper meaning.

The term, rights of an individual being discussed is the right to seek work, the right to be employed, the right to earn a decent livelihood, and the right to seek redress of valid grievances in the world of work.

Equal employment opportunity and fair employment practices intents have been executed, enacted, and promulgated through Presidential Executive Orders, laws, administrative policies and procedures at the Federal and State levels of government for the benefit of job seekers.

The following will briefly explain Presidential Executive Orders and other legislation which have been promulgated and enacted for the benefit of job seekers and employed workers, from the Federal to the State levels of government.

PRESIDENTIAL EXECUTIVE ORDERS, FEDERAL LEGISLATION, AND HAWAII STATE LAWS

Title VII of the Civil Rights Act of 1964, proclaimed a national policy of Equal Employment Opportunity in private employment for job seekers without discrimination because of race, color, religion, sex or national origin. An Amendment to Title VII, is the Equal Employment Opportunity Act of 1972. Subsequent amendments have been made.

The Age Discrimination In Employment Act of 1967 (Public Law 90-202), effective June 12, 1968, prohibits discrimination against employed workers and job applicants who are between 40 years and less than 65 years of age. This prohibition affects employers who are involved in interstate commerce. On November 28, 1975, Public Law 94-135 imposed more restrictive measures on employers who are recipients of Federal financial assistance.

Executive Order 11246 of September 24, 1965, signed by President Johnson, carried forward the program of Equal Employment Opportunity in government employment, employment by government contractors and sub-contractors, and in Federally assisted contracts without discrimination because of race, creed, color, or national origin.

Executive Order 11375 of October 13, 1967, also signed by President Johnson, Amended Order 11246 by including non-discrimination based on sex.

Provisions of these Presidential Executive Orders called for affirmative action programs which required contractors to do more than ensure employment neutrality with regard to race, color, religion, sex or national origin. Such action shall include, but not be limited to the following:

> Employment, upgrading, demotion, or transfer; recruitment or recruiting advertising; layoff or termination; rates of pay or other forms of compensation; and selection for training, including apprenticeship.

Recipients of Federal monies are required to implement affirmative action programs. As an example, the U.S. Department of Health, Education and Welfare issued guidelines to assist colleges and universities receiving Federal contracts to meet their equal employment opportunity responsibilities. These guidelines expressed the embodiment of the two concepts of Executive Order 11246, non-discrimination and affirmative action. Non-discrimination required the elimination of all existing discriminatory conditions, and mandated that policies and practices, including supervisors, be non-discriminatory in practice and action and that these did not operate to the detriment of any person on the grounds of race, color, religion, sex or national origin.

Further:

> Affirmative action requires the contractor to do more than ensure employment neutrality with regard to race, color, religion, sex, and national origin. As the phrase implies, affirmative action requires the employer to make additional efforts to recruit, employ and promote qualified members of groups formerly excluded even if that exclusion cannot be traced to particular discriminatory actions on the part of the employers. The premise of the affirmative action concept of the Executive Order is that unless positive action is undertaken to overcome the effects of systematic institutional forms of exclusion and discrimination, a benign neutrality in employment practices will tend to perpetuate the status quo ante indefinitely.

These guidelines spell out requirements relating to goals and timetables, personnel policies, placement, job classification, assignment, training, promotion, termination, conditions of work, rights and benefits-salary, back pay, leave policies, employment policies relating to pregnancy and childbirth, fringe benefits, child care, grievance procedures, and the development of affirmative action programs.

In Hawaii some progress has been made in the public colleges and university.

Guidelines for other recipients of Federal funds are required to be implemented similar to the guidelines just mentioned.

Public Law 93-508, Vietnam Era Veterans Readjustment Assistance Act of 1974, was enacted to assist Vietnam Era

Veterans in employment. Under this law, job openings under certain conditions are required to be listed with the Federal State Employment System by Federal contractors and sub-contractors. (In Hawaii, this would be the offices of the Hawaii State Employment Service.) This includes openings by Federal agencies and Federal contractors and sub-contractors (public and private) which hold contracts in the amount of $10,000 or more with Federal government agencies. Federal contractors are required to take affirmative action to employ and advance in employment qualified veterans and veterans of the Vietnam Era, in jobs in all categories which are compensated on wage or salary basis of less than $25,000. Full-time and temporary employment of more than three days' duration and part-time employment are included.

The Rehabilitation Act of 1973, Public Law 92-112, signed by President Nixon on September 26, 1973, among other things, required government contractors and sub-contractors to take affirmative action to employ and advance in employment qualified handicapped individuals. The term "handicapped individual means any person who has a physical or mental impairment which substantially limits one or more of such person's major life activities, has a record of such impairment, or is regarded as having such an impairment."[1] In other words, any person with a physical or mental disability which constitutes, or results in, a substantial barrier to employment. Under this Act, affirmative action is required of employers doing business with the Federal government with contracts of more than $2,500.00.

Act 180, Hawaii's Fair Employment Practices Law, became effective January 1, 1964. Under this law, certain discriminatory practices relating to employment on the part of employers, labor unions, employment agencies and others are considered to be illegal if such practices discriminate against persons because of race, sex, age, religion, color, or ancestry. Amendments to this law made discriminatory practices based on physical handicaps, arrest and court records, or marital status unlawful.

A provision of Act 180 forbids employers to elicit information from applicants prior to employment which directly or indirectly reflects on an individual's race, sex, age, religion, color or ancestry; or which requests information on other personal situations.

Two amendments to Act 180 were Act 30 and Act 109.

Act 30, Employment Discrimination against the handicapped, passed May 3, 1975, by the Hawaii State Legislature, among other matters made unlawful discriminatory employment practices based on "race, sex, age, religion, color, ancestry, *physical handicap*, or arrest and court record which do not have a substantial relationship to the functions and responsibilities of the prospective or continued employment, provided that an employer may refuse to hire an individual for good cause relating to the ability of the individual to perform the work in question." This law also made unlawful discriminatory practices "against any individual in compensation or in the terms, conditions, or privileges of employment because of race, sex, age, religion, color, ancestry, *physical handicap*, or arrest and court record."

Act 109, Employment Discrimination Due To Marital Status, passed May 17, 1975, by the Hawaii State Legislature, among other matters made unlawful discriminatory practices based "on race, sex, age, religion, color, ancestry, *marital status*, or arrest and court record which do not have a substantial relationship to the functions and responsibilities of the prospective or continued employment, provided that an employer may refuse to hire an individual for good cause relating to the ability of the individual to perform the work in question." This law also made unlawful discriminatory practices "against any individual in compensation or in the terms, conditions, or privileges of employment because of race, sex, age, religion, color, ancestry, *marital status*, or arrest and court record."

ENFORCEMENT AGENCIES

The following are lists of enforcement or compliance agencies for the benefit of job seekers in Hawaii. There are various offices throughout Hawaii and Federal Regional offices throughout the mainland. When in doubt as to the proper agency to consult or file a complaint with, the State and Federal enforcement offices or Civil Service agencies should be able to assist job seekers in channeling, or following through on, inquiries and complaints.

Hawaii's Enforcement Agencies

Enforcement Division (on Oahu)
Department of Labor and Industrial Relations
State of Hawaii
888 Mililani Street
Honolulu, Hawaii 96813

Hawaii District Office, Enforcement Division
Department of Labor and Industrial Relations
State of Hawaii
State Office Building
75 Aupuni Street
Hilo, Hawaii 96720

West Hawaii District Office, Enforcement Division
Department of Labor and Industrial Relations
State of Hawaii
Kealakekua, Hawaii 96750

Maui District Office, Enforcement Division
Department of Labor and Industrial Relations
State of Hawaii
State Office Building
54 High Street
Wailuku, Hawaii 96793

Kauai District Office, Enforcement Division
Department of Labor and Industrial Relations
State of Hawaii
State Office Building
3060 Eiwa Street
Lihue, Hawaii 96766

U.S. Department of Labor, Area Director
Employment Standards Administration
Wage and Hour Division
1833 Kalakaua Avenue
Honolulu, Hawaii 96815

Some Mainland and Regional Offices

Equal Employment Opportunity Commission
1390 Market Street, Room 325
San Francisco, California 94103

Employment Standards Administration
U.S. Department of Labor
450 Golden Gate Avenue, Room 10353
San Francisco, California 94102

Office of Federal Contract Compliance
U.S. Department of Labor
450 Golden Gate Avenue, Room 10341
San Francisco, California 94102

Office of Civil Rights*
U.S. Department of Health, Education and Welfare
330 Independence Avenue, S.W.
Washington, D.C. 20201

*The Office of Civil Rights has jurisdiction over Federal contracts with schools colleges, universities, hospitals and other medical, health and social service facilities.

OVERVIEW

The enactment of Equal Employment Opportunity mandates and legislation have reinforced the right of job seekers to seek work and be employed with dignity and to earn decent livelihoods befitting their status as human beings. Other influences which contributed towards worker's rights which the job seeker should recognize have been the influences of real workers' unions, social legislation, advocates of human rights, receptive Congresspersons, receptive employers, and other influences.

However, there are no absolutes in conformity or belief with the intents of Equal Employment Opportunity and Fair Employment Practices. Violations have occurred and will continue – whether intentionally or unintentionally. Compliance with these "Equal" intents vary. When variations deviate to the extent of being detrimental to the interests and welfare of the job seeker, recourses for remedies are found through the enforcement agencies and through the courts. Administrative bodies and administrative personnel have been less receptive.

Awareness and some knowledge of these mandates can assist you as a job seeker in situations where you feel that you have been treated unfairly, but action on these matters depends on the circumstances and the extent to which you pursue the issue.

It is your decision to pursue and seek remedies for unjust or discriminatory treatment received and to seek redress of valid grievances suffered through the compliance and enforcement of Equal Employment Opportunity intents.

Federal and state compliance and enforcement agencies exist to help you. Utilize these agencies.

CHAPTER 10
COMMENTARY: MINORITIES AND DISADVANTAGED

There are definitions of the terms minorities and disadvantaged which can serve as a guide for the job seeker who can benefit in jobs or training by qualifying for these categories. Some definitions relate to employment/training preferences, while others relate to equality in consideration for jobs. As an example, certain racial groups are given employment preferences based on minority or economic status,* while certain classes of people, through legislative intent, are given the right to be equally treated when applying for jobs. The basis for equal opportunity consideration in employment is based on sex, handicap status, age, marital status and other factors. However, the Federal or State civil service agencies, employment offices and enforcement agencies should be able to provide standard definitions and explanations to the job seeker.

Qualifying for a minority or disadvantaged status can be looked upon as a means for gaining entry into a job or training program. But aside from seeking information from Federal or State agencies, the job seeker can also make some kind of determination as to personal status by reference to the following discussion.

---

*While the term "non-discrimination" describes equal treatment which will be given to those of minority status, by practice, preference is given. (But this practice is not universal.)

CRITERIA USED TO CLASSIFY

For employment purposes, there appears to be more than one definition and different criteria in use for the term minority. As an example, the Hawaii State Employment Service presently categorizes the following ethnic groups as being minorities: Samoans, Hawaiians, Filipinos, Orientals, American Indians, Blacks, people classified as Spanish-Americans or having Spanish surnames, and those not classified as White or who fall in a category where information about them is not available. The Portuguese have been classified as being White, and the Puerto Ricans could be classified as White, or as a group not classified as White, or as a group where information about them is not available. A Puerto Rican, as with other individuals from other groups, could be classified individually depending upon the individual's situation. However, the basic criteria for classification for employment purposes emanate from the Federal office.

Another criterion used elsewhere to classify minorities is based on economics, or income earned. Possibly, other criteria are used by other agencies.

But generally in Hawaii, a list of protected minorities usually include Samoans, Hawaiians and Filipinos.

In Hawaii, the disadvantaged are identified in numerous ways: According to income earned, health, physical, mental, emotional condition, deprivation of social, cultural, educational aspects and other factors. Identification can be made by public or private agencies or by the individual.

Residing in the Waianae or Kalihi/Palama Model Cities areas will not provide an automatic identification of a disadvantaged status, but residents of these areas have been given employment preferences for personnel needs of the various human service programs which service residents of these areas.

The following sections will briefly discuss the substances of the terms minorities and disadvantaged.

MINORITIES AND DISADVANTAGED

These two terms, minorities and disadvantaged, have been discussed, explained and publicized, but somehow at times these terms seem to be one component and at other times seem to be entirely separate. Such expressions as "ethnic groups", "minority groups", "cultural groups", "low income", "on welfare", "handicapped", "with disabilities", "ghetto residents", "prison record", "come from a broken home", "culturally deprived", "socio-economically deprived", "mentally restored", and other expressions have been used synonomously for both these two categorical definitions and at times for one or the other. And at times, these two terms seem to include every group and class of people except one dominant racial group. The basis for categorizing these two terms seems at times to be a shifting and elusive substance. But when thought about and analyzed, these two terms can be separated and yet combined definitively.

While the term disadvantaged includes a myriad of situations relating to needs of people and is relatively simple to classify, the term minority is limited to a few factors relating to power sources and influences and is as easy to define. The term disadvantaged, as generally used, is based on income. Other human need factors may be used singularly or with income, and usage varies.

BASIC LACK OF RESOURCES OF MINORITIES

The following discussion will be an exercise in attempting to define the term minority and to separate this term from the term disadvantaged. Perhaps such a discussion can assist in shedding more light in a distinction between these two terms.

The anti-poverty and other special programs attempted to and have improved the socio-economic-educational status of many who were most in need and especially those who for years and generations lived in abject poverty and in deprived conditions. These programs also helped those who were not quite as deprived, but who were not affluent. Once these conditions were publicly brought to light and realistically recognized, implementation of these programs along with other factors made inroads towards the remedy of these adverse conditions. As the lack of certain basic resources contributed towards deprived conditions and situations other than affluency, the gradual improvement of personal and group situations brought realistic awareness of causative factors which produced less than affluent conditions; and with this awareness, a growing determination to maintain and improve personal or group status by overcoming these adverse conditions.

In a community or locale where one or more ethnic groups or classes of people lack certain resources which cause poverty and deprived conditions and contribute towards a non-affluent status quo situation--and the lack of these resources helps to perpetuate these situations, these groups or classes of people can be categorized as being minorities. They as a group, or individually, can also be potentially classed as being disadvantaged on the basis of being socio-economically deprived, culturally deprived, handicapped, residents of ghettos or blighted areas, long term unemployed, in poor health without resources, having a prison record, having low incomes, and generally being classed as being disadvantaged because of a variety of other factors.

But what were and still are the basic reasons or causes for this poverty, non-affluent status and deprivation of socio-economic-educational-health benefits in the society or community in which these less fortunate people live in that they are referred to as being minorities? What do these people lack or do not possess as a race, cultural group, or class of people so as to be classed as minorities?

Basically, these people or classes of people lack, or have been denied four important resources:

1) Lack of influence, voice or authority, in the legislative process.
2) Lack of influence, voice or authority, in the political process.

3) Lack of influence, voice or authority in the governmental administrative decision making process.
4) Lack of influence in the governmental administrative allocation of money, or in the budget decision making process.

However, assuming that a person is disadvantaged, does this make that person a minority? Let us also assume that a group or class of people is disadvantaged, but does this make them a minority group?

Only if a person comes from a group or class of people who lack the four components of influence can that person be referred to also as being a minority. And when a group of disadvantaged people lack the four components of influences, they too can also be identified as being a minority group.

When individuals, an ethnic group, and/or a class of people also meet the criteria of being disadvantaged and of lacking the four basic influences, then can these individuals and groups of people be classed also as being disadvantaged minorities.

Regardless of the interrelationship of situations, these individuals and groups do deserve societal consideration. Hopefully, the adversely severe situations which plague the minorities and disadvantaged will be minimized or remedied. But realistically viewed, these situations will be long enduring for some individuals and groups.

ARE YOU A MINORITY?

As a corollary to the comments being made here, there is an inference that while one ethnic group or class of people may be a minority in one locale, or community, this same group may not be a minority in another locale. By this reasoning, while this same group may have been a minority in a particular locale some time ago, they may no longer be a minority in that particular locale in another era, due to certain attainments. Realistically viewed, the gains made in evolvement from deprived and non-affluent conditions to betterment and the accumulation and possession of the four sources of influence have made this group "not a minority." Another group can make such similar gains toward a non-minority status.

There is a presumption that there is only one majority in a given community, but based on the line of thought just expressed, this presumption seems to be erroneous.

As further thoughts for consideration to assist job seekers in the assessment of their own situation relative to being a minority, it might be well to dwell on the ensuing matters and ask yourselves whether or not personal or group identification can be made with the following situations or with the groups of people being discussed:

* Those who are in the Hawaii State Legislature, in county government and in Congress make the laws and pass on the budget for programs and projects. Assess their authority, influence and situation.
* Those who are in public office, elective and appointive, make executive and administrative decisions and policies which affect the state and community with respect to many aspects of the lives of the residents. Assess these officials who have these executive and administrative powers.
* Those who are in public office, elective and appointive, who pass on the budget or fiscal matters and who administer these monies for the many programs, projects and services. Assess these officials and administrators, their fiscal responsibilities and their influence.
* Those who belong to the political parties; assess these people, or groups, who control, guide and/or influence the policies and power structure of these political parties.

In whatever locale, here in Hawaii or elsewhere, what interest or special groups do such people represent? What special or ethnic groups support them? Wherein lies their power base?

Think about the "control factors" of any community or locale. What gives authority and influence to certain individuals, political parties, socio-economic groups, and ethnic groups? What are the ingredients of a "power structure?" Basically, aren't these "control factors" comprised of the four resources of influence?

After analyzing these considerations, whether pertinent to job seekers in given job search situations, job seekers may be able to formulate realistic, and not historic or outdated opinions as to whether or not they fall within the meaning of the minority status being discussed by virtue of their personal or group relationship with the situations or groups of people under discussion. Thus, some kind of determination as to personal or group status can be realized – and potentially with this realization, perhaps some derivation of benefits gained.

OTHER "MINORITIES" AND "DISADVANTAGED GROUPS"

Through Federal and/or State legislative enactments, the minorities, the handicapped, the elderly, women and those with arrest and court records have been given the right to be equally treated when applying for jobs. (As the reader will remember, Federal and State laws on non-discrimination in employment were explained in Chapter 9.)

Legislation on job discrimination based on culture, religion, color and ancestry need no further explanation. Legislation on job discrimination based on sex and marital status, which can be applied to both sexes, have been oriented toward providing women with more equality in job opportunities. In addition, centers have been established to provide assistance to newly arrived immigrants.

While these categories of people mentioned seem to be all inclusive and have been given recognition for equality in job seeking through legislative enactments, or have been provided with agency assistance, other groups have not been afforded the same privilege.

"SOCIAL OUTCASTS"

Certain categories of people, whom some sectors in society look upon as being "social outcasts," have been given job seeking recognition in Hawaii through a legislative non-discrimination clause based on "arrest and court record." These people would be an ex-gambler, ex-prostitute, ex-drug dealer, ex-drug user, ex-robber, ex-sex offender and others whose records are officially on file with the law enforcement agencies. And of course, these people would be those who are sincerely attempting to find legitimate means of livelihood or a livelihood which is more acceptable by the society in which they live.

However, excluded from being given recognition for employment purposes through legislation has been such a group who is not, according to the social mores, straight - either male or female, as has been recognized throughout time. Or in other words, those who do not function biologically or attitudinally with the sex organs with which they were born. And as some can say, to function as nature intended them to function with the opposite sex. This group would include the homosexuals, transsexuals, transvestites, lesbians and others whom some segments of society look upon with disfavor.*

While some individuals within these sub-cultures are gainfully employed or seek jobs by "passing," others have been overt in their actions and "change of sex status" and may thus find more difficulty in seeking gainful and legitimate employment. The difficulty is greater when an individual is in such a sub-culture group, belongs to another "outcast" group, and lacks personal incentive in job seeking.

---

*The comments being made here are not being written as a pro and/or con issue, or to discuss the morality of the situation, but merely to restate a fact that such sub-culture groups do exist and that a means of livelihood or jobs is just as important and as much a right to them as with other job seekers.

OPTIONS AND ACTIONS

Not much can be said in suggesting ways and means to make employers more receptive – ways and means which have not been attempted, but perhaps a discussion about suggestions can be worthwhile.

Needless to say, for the job seeker who has a different sexual orientation, approach employers from the perspective of what they think you are, or what you want them to think that you are. Honesty may result in positive employer reaction. And perhaps if employers can be convinced that the job seeker's presence will not interfere with production, business profits, employee morale and positive working relationships with other employees and the business clientele, employers could be receptive to sincerity in this matter. And also perhaps emphasizing that within the work environment, social contacts and relationships will be minimized, duties and responsibilities of the job will be more than adequately fulfilled, and that sub-cultural aspects will not be initiated within the work setting.

Other options for a livelihood could be:

1) To free-lance in a given non-sexual type of employment where occupational skills and talents can be utilized.
2) To open a business in a given non-sexual type of employment.
3) To pool personal resources and specialties with others for legitimate business purposes.

Needless to say, these options are also open to any job seeker who desires more freedom and individuality in earning a livelihood.

As to those who are or who have been addicted to alcohol or drugs, statements on and proof of attendance at meetings of Narcotics Anonymous or Alcoholics Anonymous or other types of treatment may ease an employer's mind as to sincerity of rehabilitation by those addicted.

OVERVIEW

The minorities and disadvantaged, including the handicapped, aged, women and newly arrived immigrants have access to agency resources, programs and/or legislation to assist them in their quest for jobs. Difficult as it may be for many, resources do exist within the community with respect to providing assistance in employment. And when actually given the chance, these groups of people have performed well.

The physically or mentally handicapped, the aged, racial minorities, women and newly arrived immigrants and other categories of people have their job finding difficulties, but these difficulties (aside from personal problems) evolve from employers' attitudes which vary and which do not reflect attitudes from a moralistic point of view. However, the primary employer attitude encountered by an individual from any of the "outcast" sub-cultural groups is based upon morals, which evolves from an individual employer's moral values and/or of the societal morals of the times based upon attitudes on sex mores.

Some employers have been receptive to hiring job seekers from the minority groups, disadvantaged groups, women, immigrants and "outcast" sub-cultural groups, while others have not been. For individual employer reasons, jobs have been filled by individuals from these groups. Other jobs can be filled. Hopefully, with the passage of time, more employers will place more emphasis upon an individual's ability, sense of responsibility or work potential when considering job applicants for employment.

The assistance of a second party will be helpful in the situation of a physically or mentally handicapped individual, a person with an arrest and court record, an immigrant, a job seeker who belongs to a sub-cultural or "outcast" group under discussion, and others who need this type of assistance. The position of a second party assisting a job seeker is difficult enough, and the job seeker should provide the cooperation necessary and should not rely solely on this assistance for results. And while this type of assistance, legislation and resources do exist to assist people in employment, the job seeker must bear in mind that personal incentive, sincerity, positive action and consistency in job seeking attempts must exist within the individual in order to achieve more success in job searching.

AN AFTER THOUGHT

Directly related to the voiceless status of certain individuals and groups and their employment needs is the determination to exert pressures which can be brought to bear on those who can provide some relief - whether these remedies be to improve hiring practices or to provide more jobs. Concerted individual or group effort can be focused upon those who have voice, authority and influence in the community. Just as relief from deprived or non-affluent conditions for some has been slow in materializing, so too will remedies for employment needs. But such concerted efforts constitute a positive and effective step toward improving employment conditions and practices. (See Appendix B, page 172, for an illustration of possible action toward target groups which may provide avenues to partial solutions to employment needs. Sample approaches and reliefs have been listed.)

POSTSCRIPT AND PURPOSES

This handbook was written with an understanding of the relationship between an individual's self-respect and the consequent need for employment which furnishes the desired expression of the individual's very livelihood as well as life's potentials and personal goals.

It has been written with a very sincere desire to help guide the job seeker, in concentrated and comprehensive form, through the maze of the job searching process by providing the necessary practicalities and realities of job seeking, and including all of the salient aspects of job searching.

Furthermore, this handbook represents an attempt to contribute to the awareness that each individual has something substantial to offer to the world of work; to illuminate some of the obstacles which the job seeker may find barring the door to desired employment; to provide the means for application in job seeking; to provide the all-important job sources; to encourage the job seeker to keep persisting; and to assist in activating the personal desire and incentive which each individual possesses in order to achieve a state of security, satisfaction, and a sense of well-being.

You, as a job seeker, have a place in the world of work.

GOOD LUCK AND ALOHA

FOOTNOTES

Chapter 1

1. *Principal Federal Establishments in Hawaii, Guam and Pacific Areas,* Honolulu Area Office, U.S. Civil Service Commission, Honolulu, Hawaii, Rev. July 1976, and *Federal Employment Outlook Bulletin,* Hawaii and Pacific Area, *Bulletin No. 18,* October-December 1976.
2. *Federal Employment Outlook Bulletin, Bulletin No. 18.*
3. *Ibid.*
4. *Fiscal Year 1976 Workload Statistics Ending June 30, 1976,* Honolulu Area Office, U.S. Civil Service Commission.
5. *Ibid.*
6. A personal visit to the Honolulu Federal Job Information Center and examination of the bulletin boards which list all of the current job openings, October 19, 1976.
7. *Annual Report,* 1974-1975, Department of Personnel Services, State of Hawaii, Honolulu, Hawaii.
8. "Job Vacancy Announcements", Department of Personnel Services, State of Hawaii, Honolulu, Hawaii.
9. *Monthly Report,* 1975, Recruitment and Examination Division, Department of Personnel Services, State of Hawaii, Honolulu, Hawaii.
10. *Ibid.*
11. *Ibid.*
12. *Monthly Report,* 1976, Recruitment and Examination Division, Department of Personnel Services, State of Hawaii, Honolulu, Hawaii.
13. *Ibid.*
14. *Ibid.*
15. *Annual Report,* 1974-1975, Department of Personnel Services, p.3.
16. *Annual Report,* 1975-1976, Department of Personnel Services, State of Hawaii, Honolulu, Hawaii.
17. *Annual Report,* 1974-1975, Department of Personnel Services, p.3.
18. Personnel of the Office of Information and Complaints, City and County of Honolulu, Honolulu, Hawaii.
19. Personnel of the Department of Civil Service, City and County of Honolulu, Honolulu, Hawaii.
20. *Ibid.*

21. *Annual Report,* 1975-1976, Department of Civil Service, Honolulu City and County, Honolulu, Hawaii.
22. *Ibid.*
23. *Ibid.*
24. *Ibid.*
25. Personnel of the Office of Information and Complaints, Honolulu City and County.
26. *Oahu Telephone Directory,* December 1, 1976, Hawaiian Telephone Company, Honolulu, Hawaii.
27. McArdle, H. Roy, *Hawaii Career Directory, 1976-1977,* for College and University students, Placement and Career Planning Office, University of Hawaii at Manoa, Honolulu, Hawaii.
28. Day Care Licensing Unit, Public Welfare Division, Department of Social Services and Housing, State of Hawaii, Honolulu, Hawaii. (number of Day Care Centers as of November, 1976)
29. Tax Research and Planning Office, Department of Taxation, State of Hawaii, Honolulu, Hawaii.
30. *Ibid.*
31. *Ibid.*
32. *Oahu Telephone Directory,* December 1, 1976.
33. Honolulu Community Action Program, Inc., Main Office, Honolulu, Hawaii.
34. *Ibid.*
35. *Ibid.*
36. *Ibid.*

Chapter 2

1. Anton, Jane L., Russell, Michael L., "Employer Attitudes and Opinions Regarding Potential College Graduate Employees," Research Committee of the Western College Placement Association, Volume I, May, 1974, p.3.
2. Ibid., p.4.
3. Ibid., Appendix A.
4. Ibid., p.14.
5. Ibid., p.14.
6. *The Economy of Hawaii, 1976,* Annual Economic Report and Outlook, Department of Planning and Economic Development, State of Hawaii, Honolulu, Hawaii, p.12.
7. *Ibid., p.2.*
8. *Ibid., p.12.*
9. *Ibid., p.13.*
10. *Ibid., p.13.*
11. *Subarea Review,* July-September, 1975-1976, Research and Statistics Office, Department of Labor and Industrial Relations, State of Hawaii, Honolulu, Hawaii, June 1976, p.25.
12. *The Economy of Hawaii, 1976,* Department of Planning and Economic Development, p.19.
13. *Ibid., p.19.*
14. *Ibid., p.2.*
15. *Ibid., p.21.*
16. *Subarea Review,* July-September, 1975-1976, p.25.

17. *The Economy of Hawaii, 1976,* Department of Planning and Economic Development, p.13.
18. *Annual Planning Report,* Fiscal Year 1977, State of Hawaii and Honolulu SMSA, Department of Labor and Industrial Relations, State of Hawaii, Honolulu, Hawaii, May, 1976, p.10.
19. *The Economy of Hawaii, 1976,* Department of Planning and Economic Development, p.31.
20. *Ibid., p.13.*
21. *Ibid., p.55.*
22. *Ibid., p.55.*
23. *Ibid., p.55.*
24. *Subarea Review,* July-September, 1975-1976, p.25.
25. *The Economy of Hawaii, 1976,* Department of Planning and Economic Development, p.55.
26. *Ibid., p.56.*
27. *Ibid., p.56.*
28. *Ibid., p.56.*
29. *Ibid., p.56.*
30. *Subarea Review,* July-September, 1975-1976, p.25.
31. *Annual Planning Report,* Fiscal Year 1977, Department of Labor and Industrial Relations, p.10.
32. *Ibid., p.10.*
33. *Ibid., p.10.*
34. *Occupational Employment Trends,* Report on Labor Market Conditions for Selected Occupations, Quarterly Report, Outlook for July through September, 1976, State of Hawaii; Research and Statistics Office, Department of Labor and Industrial Relations, State of Hawaii, Honolulu, Hawaii, July 1976, p.6.
35. *Hawaii-Honolulu Area Manpower Review, 1975-1976,* Research and Statistics Office, Department of Labor and Industrial Relations, State of Hawaii, Honolulu, Hawaii, September, 1975, p.21.
36. *Ibid., p.21.*
37. *Occupational Outlook Handbook,* 1976-1977 Edition, United States Department of Labor, United States Government Printing Office, Washington, D.C., pp.207, 209 and 211.
38. *Ibid., p.211.*
39. *Ibid., p.513.*
40. *Annual Planning Report,* Fiscal Year 1977, Department of Labor and Industrial Relations, p.15.
41. *Occupational Outlook Handbook,* p.81.
42. *Annual Planning Report,* Fiscal Year 1977, Department of Labor and Industrial Relations, p.15.
43. *Ibid., p.15.*
44. *Ibid., p.15.*
45. *Ibid., p.15.*
46. *Hawaii-Honolulu Area Manpower Review, 1975-1976, p.21.*
47. *Ibid., pp.19 and 20.*
48. *Subarea Review,* July-September, 1975-1976, pp.19 and 20.
49. *Pay Rates In Hawaii,* Hawaii Employers Council Research Report - Special Publication No. 128, Honolulu, Hawaii, October, 1976.
50. *Ibid., p.1.*
51. *Ibid., p.3.*
52. *Ibid., p.1.*

53. *Ibid., p.1.*
54. *Ibid., p.3.*
55. *Ibid., p.1.*
56. *Ibid., p. 1 or 2.*
57. *Ibid., p.118.*
58. *Ibid., p.145.*
59. *Labor Force Estimate Reports,* Research and Statistics Office, Department of Labor and Industrial Relations, State of Hawaii, Honolulu, Hawaii.
60. *Ibid.*
61. *Ibid.*
62. *Ibid.*
63. *Hawaii-Honolulu Area Manpower Review, 1975-1976, p.6.*
64. *Ibid., p.26.*
65. *Labor Force Estimate Reports.*
66. *Federal Civilian Manpower Statistics,* Monthly Release, U.S. Civil Service Commission, Bureau of Manpower Information Systems, January, 1977, p.36.
67. *Ibid., p.36.*
68. *Annual Report,* 1975-1976, Department of Civil Service, Honolulu City and County, p.67.
69. *Ibid.*
70. *Annual Report,* 1975-1976, Department of Personnel Services, State of Hawaii, p.11.
71. *Hawaii's Scientific Resources,* 1974-1975 Directory, Seventh Edition, Department of Planning and Economic Development, State of Hawaii, Honolulu, Hawaii, p.8.
72. *Ibid., p.9.*
73. *Women Workers in Hawaii,* Research and Statistics Office, Department of Labor and Industrial Relations, State of Hawaii, Honolulu, Hawaii.
74. *Ibid.*
75. *Ibid., p.21.*
76. *Hawaii's Scientific Resources,* 1974-1975, p.4.
77. *Labor Market Indicators, 1970-1976,* Research and Statistics Office, Department of Labor and Industrial Relations, State of Hawaii, Honolulu, Hawaii, August, 1976.
78. *Labor Force Estimate Reports.*
79. *Ibid.*
80. *Ibid.*
81. *Ibid.*
82. *Ibid.*
83. *Ibid.*
84. *Hawaii-Honolulu Area Manpower Review,* 1975-1976, p.7.
85. *Labor Area Summary,* Research and Statistics Office, Department of Labor and Industrial Relations, State of Hawaii, Honolulu, Hawaii, September, 1976.
86. *Ibid.*
87. *Agreement* between the Hotels and the Hotel, Restaurant Employees and Bartenders' Union, Local 5, AFL-CIO, June 1, 1975 to May 31, 1977, Honolulu, Hawaii.

Chapter 3

1. *Licensed Occupations in Hawaii,* Research and Statistics Office, Department of Labor and Industrial Relations, State of Hawaii, Honolulu, Hawaii, 96813, February, 1975, p.9.
2. *Starting A Business in Hawaii,* Fifth Edition, Published by the Department of Planning and Economic Development, State of Hawaii, Honolulu, Hawaii, 96813, 1976.
3. *Licensed Occupations in Hawaii.*
4. *Rule 15, Admission to the Bar,* Supreme Court of Hawaii, Honolulu, Hawaii.
5. *Dictionary Of Occupational Titles,* Volume I, Definitions of Titles, Third Edition, U.S. Department of Labor, 1965, p.xv.

Chapter 4

1. Rosenberg, Carl, "Job Seeking Methods Used By American Workers", *Monthly Labor Review,* Bureau of Labor Statistics, U.S. Department of Labor, August, 1975, p.39.
2. *Ibid., p.39.*
3. *Ibid., p.39.*
4. *Ibid., p.40.*
5. *Ibid., p.40.*
6. *Ibid., p.42.*
7. *Ibid., p.42.*
8. *Ibid., p.42.*
9. *Ibid., p.42.*
10. Ibid., p.42.
11. Ibid., p.39.

Chapter 5

1. *Military/Civilian Occupational Source Book,* First Edition, Department of Defense, United States; prepared by the Armed Forces Vocational Testing Group, Universal City, Texas, July 1975.
2. *Dictionary of Occupational Titles,* Volume II, Occupational Classification, Third Edition, U.S. Department of Labor, 1965, p.649.
3. *Ibid., p.649.*
4. *Ibid., p.649.*
5. *Ibid., p.651.*
6. *Ibid., p.651.*
7. *Ibid., pp.217 to 529.*
8. *Ibid., pp.217 to 529.*
9. *Ibid., pp.243 to 292.*
10. *Ibid., pp.217 to 529.*

Chapter 6

1. Won, Greta C., *Gambling With Speech,* Vi-Tel Publications, Honolulu, Hawaii, 1972, p.26.
2. *Employment Practices Law,* Hawaii Revised Statutes, Chapter 378, State of Hawaii.

3. *Ibid.*
4. Won, Greta C., *Gambling With Speech,* p.204.
5. *Ibid., p.205.*
6. *Ibid., p.205.*
7. *Ibid., p.205.*
8. *Ibid., p.99.*
9. *Ibid., p.211.*
10. *Ibid., p.213.*

Chapter 7

1. *Won, Greta C.,* Gambling With Speech, p.215.

Chapter 8

1. *Hawaii-Honolulu Area Manpower Review,* 1975-1976, p.20.;
2. *Annual Planning Report,* Fiscal Year 1977, Department of Labor and Industrial Relations, pp.27 and 28.

Chapter 9

1. *Affirmative Action Regulations On Handicapped Workers,* U.S. Department of Labor, August 22, 1975, p.3.

Appendix A

1. *Employment Service Automated Reporting System, 1975-1976,* Hawaii State Employment Service, Department of Labor and Industrial Relations, State of Hawaii, Honolulu, Hawaii.
2. *Ibid.*
3. *Ibid.*
4. *Labor Area Summary,* Research and Statistics Office, Department of Labor and Industrial Relations, State of Hawaii, Honolulu, Hawaii, July , 1976.
5. *Employment Service Automated Reporting System, 1974-1975,* Hawaii State Employment Service, Department of Labor and Industrial Relations, State of Hawaii, Honolulu, Hawaii.
6. *Ibid.*

BIBLIOGRAPHY

Affirmative Action Regulations on Handicapped Workers, U. S. Department of Labor, August 22, 1975.

Agreement between the Hotels and Hotel, Restaurant Employees and Bartenders' Union, Local 5, AFL-CIO, June 1, 1975, to May 31, 1977, Honolulu, Hawaii.

Annual Planning Report, Fiscal Year 1977, State of Hawaii and Honolulu SMSA, Department of Labor and Industrial Relations, State of Hawaii, Honolulu, Hawaii, May, 1976.

Annual Report, 1975-1976, Department of Civil Service, Honolulu City and County, Honolulu, Hawaii.

Annual Report, 1974-1975, Department of Personnel Services, State of Hawaii, Honolulu, Hawaii.

Annual Report, 1975-1976, Department of Personnel Services, State of Hawaii, Honolulu, Hawaii.

Anton, Jane L., Russell, Michael L., "Employer Attitudes and Opinions Regarding Potential College Graduate Employees," Research Committee of the Western College Placement Association, Volume I, May, 1974.

Day Care Licensing Unit, Public Welfare Division, Department of Social Services and Housing, State of Hawaii, Honolulu, Hawaii.

Dictionary of Occupational Titles, Volume I, Definitions of Titles, Third Edition, U.S. Department of Labor, 1965.

Dictionary Of Occupational Titles, Volume II, Occupational Classifications, Third Edition, U.S. Department of Labor, 1965.

Economy Of Hawaii, The, 1976, Annual Economic Report and Outlook, Department of Planning and Economic Development, State of Hawaii, Honolulu, Hawaii.

Employment Practices Law, Hawaii Revised Statutes, Chapter 378, State of Hawaii, Honolulu, Hawaii.

Employment Service Automated Reporting System, 1974-1975, Hawaii State Employment Service, Department of Labor and Industrial Relations, State of Hawaii, Honolulu, Hawaii.

Employment Service Automated Reporting System, 1975-1976, Hawaii State Employment Service, Department of Labor and Industrial Relations, State of Hawaii, Honolulu, Hawaii.

Federal Civilian Manpower Statistics, Monthly Release, U.S. Civil Service Commission, Bureau of Manpower Information Systems, January, 1977.

Federal Employment Outlook Bulletin, Hawaii and Pacific Area, Bulletin No. 18, October-December, 1976.

Fiscal Year 1976 Workload Statistics Ending June 30, 1976, Honolulu Area Office, U.S. Civil Service Commission.

Hawaii-Honolulu Area Manpower Review, 1975-1976, Research and Statistics Office, Department of Labor and Industrial Relations, State of Hawaii, Honolulu, Hawaii, September, 1975.

Hawaii's Scientific Resources, 1974-1975 Directory, Seventh Edition, Department of Planning and Economic Development, State of Hawaii, Honolulu, Hawaii.

Honolulu Community Action Program, Inc., Main Office, Honolulu, Hawaii.

"Job Vacancy Announcements", Department of Personnel Services, State of Hawaii, Honolulu, Hawaii.

Labor Area Summary, Research and Statistics Office, Department of Labor and Industrial Relations, State of Hawaii, Honolulu, Hawaii, July, 1976.

Labor Area Summary, Research and Statistics Office, Department of Labor and Industrial Relations, State of Hawaii, Honolulu, Hawaii, September, 1976.

Labor Force Estimate Reports, Research and Statistics Office, Department of Labor and Industrial Relations, State of Hawaii, Honolulu, Hawaii.

Labor Market Indicators, 1970-1976, Research and Statistics Office, Department of Labor and Industrial Relations, State of Hawaii, Honolulu, Hawaii, August, 1976.

Licensed Occupations In Hawaii, Research and Statistics Office, Department of Labor and Industrial Relations, State of Hawaii, Honolulu, Hawaii, February, 1975.

Manoa Campus Bulletin, Weekly Publication, University of Hawaii at Manoa, Honolulu, Hawaii.

McArdle, H. Roy, *Hawaii Career Directory, 1976-1977,* for College and University students, Placement and Career Planning Office, University of Hawaii at Manoa, Honolulu, Hawaii.

Military/Civilian Occupational Source Book, First Edition, Department of Defense, United States; prepared by the Armed Forces Vocational Testing Group, Universal City, Texas, July, 1975.

Monthly Report, 1975, Recruitment and Examination Division, Department of Personnel Services, State of Hawaii, Honolulu, Hawaii.

Monthly Report, 1976, Recruitment and Examination Division, Department of Personnel Services, State of Hawaii, Honolulu, Hawaii.

Oahu Telephone Directory, Hawaiian Telephone Company, Honolulu, Hawaii, December 1, 1976.

Occupational Employment Trends, Report on Labor Market Conditions for Selected Occupations, Quarterly Report, Outlook for July through September, 1976; Research and Statistics Office, Department of Labor and Industrial Relations, State of Hawaii, Honolulu, Hawaii, July, 1976.

Occupational Outlook Handbook, 1976-1977 Edition, United States Department of Labor, United States Government Printing Office, Washington, D.C.

Pay Rates In Hawaii, Hawaii Employers Council, Research Report - Special Publication No. 128, Honolulu, Hawaii, October, 1976.

Personal visit to the Honolulu Federal Job Information Center and examination of the bulletin boards which list all of the current job openings, October 19, 1976.

Personnel of the Department of Civil Service, Honolulu City and County, Honolulu, Hawaii.

Personnel of the Office of Information and Complaints, Honolulu City and County, Honolulu, Hawaii.

Principal Federal Establishments in Hawaii, Guam and Pacific Areas, Honolulu Area Office, U.S. Civil Service Commission, Honolulu, Hawaii, Rev. July, 1976.

Rosenberg, Carl, "Job Seeking Methods Used By American Workers", *Monthly Labor Review,* Bureau of Labor Statistics, U.S. Department of Labor, August, 1975.

Rule 15, Admission To The Bar, Supreme Court of Hawaii, Honolulu, Hawaii.

Starting A Business In Hawaii, Fifth Edition, Published by the Department of Planning and Economic Development, State of Hawaii, Honolulu, Hawaii, 1976.

Subarea Review, July-September, 1975-1976, Research and Statistics Office, Department of Labor and Industrial Relations, State of Hawaii, Honolulu, Hawaii, June, 1976.

Tax Research and Planning Office, Department of Taxation, State of Hawaii, Honolulu, Hawaii.

Women Workers In Hawaii, Research and Statistics Office, Department of Labor and Industrial Relations, State of Hawaii, Honolulu, Hawaii.

Won, Greta C., *Gambling With Speech,* Vi-Tel Publications, Honolulu, Hawaii, 1972.

Other References

Annual Report, Department of Labor and Industrial Relations, State of Hawaii, Honolulu, Hawaii.

Annual Report, Department of Planning and Economic Development, State of Hawaii, Honolulu, Hawaii.

Annual Report To The Governor, Prepared jointly by the Commission on Manpower and Full Employment and the State Manpower Services Council, State of Hawaii, Honolulu, Hawaii.

Checklist Of Labor Market Information, Research and Statistics Office, Department of Labor and Industrial Relations, State of Hawaii, Honolulu, Hawaii.

College Placement Annual, College Placement Council, Inc., Bethlehem, Pennsylvania. (annual publication)

Directory of Libraries and Information Sources in Hawaii and The Pacific Islands, The, Bi-Annual Publication of the Hawaii Library Association, Honolulu, Hawaii.

Employment and Payrolls in Hawaii, Research and Statistics Office, Department of Labor and Industrial Relations, State of Hawaii, Honolulu, Hawaii. (annual report)

Energy Resources Coordinator, Department of Planning and Economic Development, State of Hawaii, Honolulu, Hawaii. (annual report)

Federal Career Directory, U.S. Civil Service Commission, Washington, D.C. (periodic revisions)

Guide to Occupations in Hawaii, A, (8 volumes), Career Information Center, Office of the State Director for Vocational Education, University of Hawaii, Honolulu, Hawaii.

Hawaii And The Sea, Report of the Governor's Committee on Science and Technology; Department of Planning and Economic Development, State of Hawaii, Honolulu, Hawaii, February 11, 1974.

Interindustry Study Of The Hawaiian Economy, Research and Economic Analysis Division, Department of Planning and Economic Development, State of Hawaii, Honolulu, Hawaii, 1972.

Labor Force Information for Affirmative Action Programs, Research and Statistics Office, Department of Labor and Industrial Relations, State of Hawaii, Honolulu, Hawaii.

Pacific Business News, Honolulu, Hawaii. (weekly publication)

State of Hawaii Data Book, The, Department of Planning and Economic Development, State of Hawaii, Honolulu, Hawaii. (annual publication)

Tourism in Hawaii, Volume I, Department of Planning and Economic Development, State of Hawaii, Honolulu, Hawaii, 1972.

Unfilled Job Openings Report, Research and Statistics Office, Department of Labor and Industrial Relations, State of Hawaii, Honolulu, Hawaii. (periodic publication)

Wage Rate Schedule Bulletin (Public Construction Work), Department of Labor and Industrial Relations, State of Hawaii, Honolulu, Hawaii.

APPENDIX A

DATA ON APPLICANTS SERVED AND JOB PLACEMENTS MADE BY PERSONNEL OF THE HAWAII STATE EMPLOYMENT SERVICE DURING THE 1974-1975 and 1975-1976 FISCAL YEARS

During the 1975-1976 fiscal year, there were 123,559 available and registered job applicants with the Hawaii State Employment Service; from this number, 20,688 individual job placements were made.[1] If the number of placement and individuals placed in jobs more than once during this period are included, there were 24,824 job placements or transactions.[2] New applications and renewals during this period numbered 93,415.[3] During this period, women comprised 45% of all job applicants seeking work through this agency.[4]

During the previous fiscal year, 1974-1975, there were 104,677 job applicants available and registered for work with this state agency.[5] Of these, 19,870 were placed in jobs by personnel of this state agency during this period.[6]

Appendix B

POSSIBLE GROUP ACTION TO PROVIDE PARTIAL RELIEF FOR EMPLOYMENT NEEDS

Group and Individual Needs	Target Groups	Possible Approaches	Employment Reliefs Desired
Decent Jobs and Security	State Government Representatives and Administrators	Community or Group Pressure; Encourage Legislation; Use Political Action	Creation of Jobs Equality in Hiring Practices
Decent Jobs and Security	County Government Representatives and Administrators	Utilization of Personnel to Advocate Improvement in Employment Condtions; Use Political Action	Improvement in Employment Laws
Decent Jobs and Security	Congressional Representatives	Group and/or Individual Contacts, Petition, or Corresdences; Use Political Action	Mandatory Public Advertisement of Governmental Jobs
Decent Jobs and Security	Private Industry	Approach Influential Organizations and and Large Companies	More Subsidy of Jobs and Training in Government and Private Industry

APPENDIX C

CAREER PLACEMENT
Practicalities and Realities

Outline for a one-credit course taught
at Leeward Community College by the Author

Course Description
Preparations for job seeking and placement: A survey of general labor market conditions and trends, job sources, employers, students' abilities and potentials, human relations, importance of job interviews and approaches, job seeking methods, applications, letters, resumes, self-assesment, self-inventory, motivation, persistence, factors which create barriers to employment, and Equal Employment Opportunity Laws.

Course Goals
To assist students realistically and systematically to seek out employment and cope with the competition in the job market.

1) To help students acquire knowledge of in-depth job search techniques and preparations.
2) To help students apply knowledge of in-depth job search techniques and preparations, in order that they can better help themselves to seek and hold jobs.

Text - *Job Searching in Hawaii,* Adam P.Y. Lim, 1977, Revised.
Reading, Reference Materials — Assigned Materials.
Prerequisites - None

Grading
There will be a determined number of short quizzes to be administered during class periods. There will also be three take-home assignments to be completed in writing. The three

take-home assignments and the class quizzes will be graded. Each student will be graded on the basis of zero to 100% in each of the class quizzes and take-home assignments, and the accumulated percentage points will be averaged to determine the final grade for each student.

Examination dates will be given on the first and second day of classes. Due dates for the written assignments will also be given.

The student will be graded individually on the basis of number of assignments completed and accuracy on quizzes. The percentage scale and equivalent letter grades for quizzes and assignments are given below:

90 - 100% A
80 - 89% B
70 - 79% C
60 - 69% D
Below 60% W or N

Make-up Examinations

Each student will be given an opportunity to retake the written quizzes to upgrade his/her percentage. However, arrangements of time will be the responsibility of the student. Make-ups should be done within a week of the examinations.

Class Attendance

It is very important to attend classes regularly. The scope of this short term course is sufficiently broad and diverse that no student can expect to fully grasp the significance of the contents without regular attendance.

UNIT OBJECTIVES

Unit 1 Labor Market Information (one class period)

Given informational materials, reference sources and class discussions, each student will acquire knowledge and develop an understanding of labor market conditions and employment trends as they pertain to him/her. He/she will be apprised of the sources from which information about these areas can be obtained.

Specifically the student will, based on assigned readings, reference materials and class discussions:

1) Identify two upward employment trends relative to his/her interests. 20%
2) List four job turnover factors or conditions that create or cause job openings. 20%
3) Identify two demand or publicized occupations relative to his/her interests. 30%
4) Give a pay rate range of two jobs relative to his/her interests. 10%
5) Identify four sources which give information on labor market conditions and employment trends, giving source of his/her information or the publication(s). 20%

Unit 2 Job Sources (one class period)
Given informational materials, sources, and class discussions the student will acquire knowledge and develop an understanding of specific job sources and training programs as they pertain to his/her immediate and future job interests, and be able to identify the three governmental civil service agencies by name and location.

Specifically the student will, based on assigned readings, reference materials, and class discussions:

1) Give the names and locations of the three governmental civil service agencies in Hawaii and one non-civil service Federal governmental agency. 20%
2) Name two training programs or two jobs by title currently available in any of the three civil service agencies relative to his/her job interests. 10%
3) List three special employability services or programs offered by the Hawaii State Employment Service based on discussions in class or on assigned reference materials. 30%
4) List correctly by name four major private companies located on Oahu, with more than 100 employees. 20%

5) Identify, other than the civil service agencies and private firms, four other sources where job opening information can be obtained. 20%

Unit 3 About Employers (one class period)
Given informational materials and class discussions, the student will acquire knowledge and develop an understanding of employers' expectations relative to advertising job openings, reasons for hiring, competitiveness of jobs, selectivity, and the importance of human relations and work potential in the job market. Specifically the student will, based on class discussions and/or assigned materials:

1) List two methods of publicizing jobs commonly used by employers. 10%
2) List three reasons or basis, which employers practice or utilize, to hire or select employees. 15%
3) List three positive work traits desired by employers. 15%
4) State two reasons why competitiveness for jobs in the labor market is an advantage to employers. 10%
5) Identify ten positive personal characteristics or traits of prospective employees which are considered to be important by employers. 50%

Unit 4 Self-assessment, Self-inventory, Application and Motivation (one class period)
Given informational materials, group interaction and discussions, the student will acquire knowledge and develop an understanding of the self-assessment and self-inventory processes as factors in job seeking. Specifically, the student will undergo a self-assessment process of:

1) Personal qualities and values. 25%
2) How employers perceive the student. 25%

The student will also undergo a self-inventory process of:

1) Personal work experiences, skills, knowledges and potentials - civilian and military. 25%

2) Personal past-life experiences gained, unrelated to employment. 25%

Positive application and motivational aspects of the student will also be discussed.

Unit 5 Resumes, Letters, Applications and Other Documents (two class periods)

Given informational materials, group interaction and discussions, the student will acquire knowledge and develop an understanding of the means and importance of adequately preparing and filling out applications, resumes, letters and other documents as preparations for employment. Specifically, the student will, based on class discussions and readings:

1) List two important reasons why job applicants must fill out application blanks legibly and completely as possible. 10%
2) State in one sentence a basic purpose of a resume. 10%
3) List at least ten salient points pertaining to his/her previous work/educational experiences and/or personal abilities or potential which can be applied to a specific job interest. 50%
4) List six types of documents or materials which can be used to submit to employers in order to enhance the job seeker's chances for employment. 30%

Assignments

1) Prepare and submit a personal resume.
2) Prepare and write a letter of application to a company or agency for a specific job.

Unit 6 Job Interviews (two class periods)

Given informational materials, class discussions and analysis of live job interviews coupled with listening to tapes, the student will acquire knowledge and develop an understanding of the practicality and importance of proper approaches, conduct, appearance and ready answers in job interviews. Specifically, the student will, based on discussions in class and/or assigned materials:

1) List five procedures or preparations considered important prior to or when arranging for job interviews. 25%
2) Identify five positive behavioral factors in job interviews. 25%
3) Identify five non-positive or negative behavioral factors in job interviews. 25%
4) List five difficult questions generally asked in job interviews. 25%

Unit 7 Barriers to Employment (one class period)
Through informational materials and discussions, the student will develop an understanding of the barriers to employment and endeavor to minimize or overcome these barriers. Specifically, the student will, based on class discussions and assigned reference readings:

1) List five specific or potential personal barriers to employment in short phrases or sentences as these pertain to his/her immediate or long range job interest. 50%
2) List one possible solution for each of the five specific barriers to employment you have listed. 50%

Unit 8 Equal Employment Opportunity Laws (one class period)
Through information and class discussions, the student will acquire knowledge and develop an understanding of Equal Employment Opportunity Laws and enforcement agencies as they relate to job seeking and remedies sought and be able to identify:

1) Two basic Federal employment laws, by title. 20%
2) Two basic Hawaii State employment laws, by title. 20%
3) Two Federal enforcement agencies on the mainland, by name. 20%

4) Two enforcement agencies in Hawaii, by name. 20%
5) Two racial minority groups which are given employment preferences by law 20%

Unit 9 The Job Search (one class period)
Given informational materials and through class discussions, the student will acquire knowledge and develop an understanding of the steps which need to be taken in seeking a job up to the point of the actual job interview. Specifically, the student will:

1) Write a one or two-page narrative report on his/her plan of action for a job hunt based on knowledge acquired from past discussions and reference materials. The report will include and make reference to:
   a) job informational sources. 25%
   b) specific job openings by job titles. 25%
   c) arranging for job interviews. 50%

Assignment
To write on a plan of action for a job hunt.

Unit 10 Persistence in Job Seeking and Review of Course (one class period)
Through discussions, the student will gain an appreciation of the importance of persistency in the search for a job. Specifically, the student will, based on class discussions:

1) List two reasons why persistency is important in the search for a job. 10%
2) List three attitudinal or personal non-positive factors which deters an individual from being persistent in his/her job search. 15%

Assignments to be turned in:
1) Turn in letter of application. 25%
2) Turn in personal resume. 50%

There will also be an overall review and discussion of Job Search Preparations before the final examination.